THE REAL
OWNERS OF
BRITAIN

THE REAL OWNERS OF BRITAIN

HOW STOCKHOLM SYNDROME
AND TRANS-GENERATIONAL
TRAUMA CAN BE TRACED AMONG
IMMIGRANTS IN BRITAIN

ONYEKA NWELUE

New York & London

First published in Great Britain in 2022
by Abibiman Publishing

First published in India in 2022 by
Abibiman Publishing India
www.abibimanpublishing.com

ISBN: 978-1739774776

This is a work of non-fiction.

Cover design: Fred Martins & George Syphar
Illustrations by Frank Anwuacha

for

Seun Kuti, *and my other soldiers*:
Adeleke Togun
Mishael Maro Amos
Ebuka Ifeanyi Iloegbunam
Aboyeji Iyinoluwa
Obiora Anozie
Aneto Emeka Chukwuka

ABOUT THE AUTHOR

Onyeka Nwelue is the founder of the Oxford-based James Currey Society.

A filmmaker and author of over 11 award-winning books, he is a member of The Oxford Union Society, a debating society in the city of Oxford, England, whose membership is drawn primarily from the University of Oxford.

His non-fiction book, *Hip-Hop is Only for Children* won the Creative Non-Fiction Book of the Year at the 2015 Nigerian Writers' Awards. He studied Sociology & Anthropology at the University of Nigeria, Nsukka and Directing at Prague Film School in Czech Republic. He was awarded an Honorary Doctor of Humane Letters, by Universite Queensland in Haiti.

He studied Ancient Masterpieces of World Literature at Harvard University and Business of Music at Berklee College of Music in Boston.

He was an Associate Research Fellow at the University of Johannesburg. He was a Visiting Research Fellow at the Center for International Studies, Ohio University.

He is currently a visiting assistant professor and Visiting Fellow of African Literature and studies in the English Language Department of the Faculty of Humanities, Manipur University in Imphal, India.

He is an Academic Visitor at the African Studies Centre, University of Oxford.

He splits his time between Oxford and Johannesburg.

CONTENTS

OPENING NOTE

Money is power. When you have power, it can be intoxicating. That is why the power gate-keepers that money spawn like to delight in the broth of infallibility.

But when powerful people are dragooned to their knees, it is always disastrous.

Let's think of Harvey Weinstein—who was the Executive Producer of almost every film you could find on Netflix, when they started. He provided them with all sorts of mooi content as you'd imagine. Still and all when his time was up, his fall was deep, steep, and tragic.

Harvey had the money, so he had the power. Money is magnetic. It brings close to you, the wrong people. As you have the money, you have the power. There are many people hanging around to demystify you and wring that power away from you, for themselves. Every powerful person, has someone, willing to take him out.

In the circle of the powerful, it is the least powerful that wants to usurp all the powers. They stay strategically placing themselves where they can take over.

The real owners of Britain are not the 'real' Britons. The real owners of Britain are people, whose ancestors came here long ago. They have now mastered the channels to get to where they want and when they do, they no longer want others, who look like them to come in.

Just like the poor who, on becoming rich, will leave their poor neighborhood and move into a wealthy one and protect themselves from the poor, whom they had left behind.

Here are the dynamics of money and how money translates to wealth and rips your heart apart. This is the same about how people buckle and control narratives; they want people to see the world the way they see it and live by the rules created by them.

There are people who want to revolutionise things but they end up, looking like momparas.

I remember when I approached German anthropologist, Dr. Sabine Jell-Bahlsen, to write a Foreword to this book, she said to me in her email: "I have just read your intro to the book and found it very confusing. I must admit that I am neither aware of the Akwaeze--Adichie debate, nor have I seen Akwaeze's face on *Time* (magazine?), nor have I read your piece in the Lagos review."

She continued, "Also, my take on Ogbanje is somewhat different. I have come to regard Ogbanje as "children who torture their parents by always die-ing and returning to life on earth." (Chinwe Achebe, World of the Ogbanje)."

She added, "When I was afraid of a child's Ogbanje fate, I asked the late Eze Mmiri, Madame Martha Mberekpe of Orsu-Obodo about this. She had lost 11 children, all of her sons. The woman lost her mind when losing so many children. She became insane, was healed by the late Ebiri Obua, and initiated into the worship of the Water Goddess, Ogbuide, and her husband, Urashi. The late Eze Nwanyi Akkuzor of Oguta was a follower, (healed and initiated) by the Eze Mmiri (Mberekpe). The Eze Mmiri (Mberekpe) told me that the connection between Ogbuide or Urashi and Ogbanje is this: "When a person dies, he or she must face the Water God/dess before reincarnation. Since Ogbanje is frequently re-incarnating, they will always face the Water God/dess before returning to earth. However, the Water Goddess does not cause a person to be Ogbanje; they just meet in the process."

Dr. Sabine understands how narratives shape our thoughts: "The Eze Mmiri was appalled by "Mammy Water scares spread by Christian proselytes. They claim that Mammy Water/ the Water Goddess turns people into Ogbanje." The priestess said, "That is a lie."

"An example was the Mammy Water scare at Enugu in 1990. It's in my book," she added. "In any event, Ogbanje is a fate, not a person's willful making. The claim of the Akwaeke woman you describe sounds unfathomable, preposterous, or perhaps extremely provocative, debased, or alienated from their own history. I don't understand her and I am now curious and looking forward to reading how the introduction connects to your story. Thanks for sharing."

She gave me permission to quote her by reproducing this. This is why I have chosen to open this book the way I am about to.

Let's see if the introduction connects to my story

On March 12th, 2022, someone called my attention to social media posts made by Dr. Shashi Tharoor about meeting me. This beautiful mind gave me so much visibility to his over 2 million followers.

This is the post:

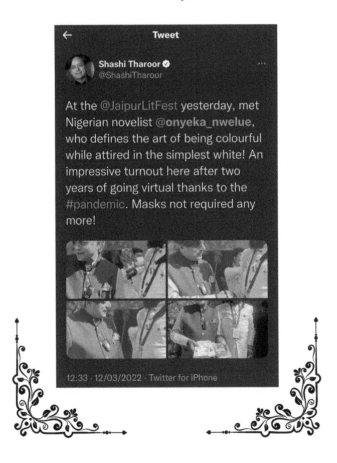

Tweet

Shashi Tharoor ✓
@ShashiTharoor

At the @JaipurLitFest yesterday, met Nigerian novelist @onyeka_nwelue, who defines the art of being colourful while attired in the simplest white! An impressive turnout here after two years of going virtual thanks to the #pandemic. Masks not required any more!

12:33 · 12/03/2022 · Twitter for iPhone

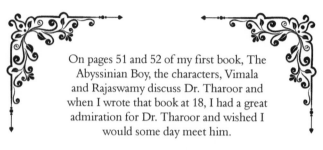

On pages 51 and 52 of my first book, The Abyssinian Boy, the characters, Vimala and Rajaswamy discuss Dr. Tharoor and when I wrote that book at 18, I had a great admiration for Dr. Tharoor and wished I would some day meet him.

At the Jaipur Literature Festival in 2022, I had a session with the Turkish Ambassador to India, Mr. Firat Sunel at 1pm and Dr. Tharoor was having one with William Darylmple at 2pm. As soon as I finished my session, I ran off to watch Dr. Tharoor.

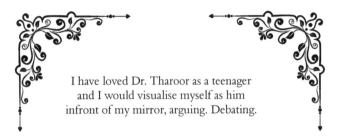

I have loved Dr. Tharoor as a teenager
and I would visualise myself as him
infront of my mirror, arguing. Debating.

So, meeting him, solidified my dream
and I do hope that, in this book, you'd
discover how much of an influence he
has been.

I want you to enjoy the entire book as
much as I did, writing it.

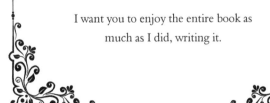

INTRODUCTION

"The truth will set you free, but first it will piss you off."
- Gloria Steinem

May I remind you, that most of the arguments here, have been published elsewhere.

My take on Ms Adichie and Akwaeke, was published on The Lagos Review, but I am going to reproduce it, before I begin to talk about other important things. Reason being, that discussing these two, will bring you hate. This is why it should be discussed, to defy the arrogance of cancel culture and clip the wings of its crusaders.

People say people should take responsibilities for what they do. I agree, totally and it is why I want to talk about this again. It might be really great to know the kind of era we are in now, and let people know the reign of crookedness is over.

Akwaeke mutilated herself and claimed they are ogbanje. How brazen!

The Igbo/Tamil writer Akwaeke Emezi is not Ogbanje. They were not born Ogbanje—and one can't decide, on a whim, that they are ogbanje, except they suffer from an obsessive European disease that has no cure. Simply put, that isn't how it works.

Igbo cosmology does not allow the gormless leap from sexual identity or surgical transitions to Ogbanje. Claiming that it does is deceitful and obnoxious.

In one of Emezi's emails to Chimamanda Ngozi Adichie, they confessed not knowing how to speak or write Igbo. But, somehow, to oil the wheels of their self-obsessed chicanery, and certainly for European appeal, they had the temerity to publicly corrupt a deeply complicated cultural gnosis, which even those with profound understanding of the Igbo language and culture discuss only with reverence. How do we trust such people's sudden omniscience when they themselves are lacking in requisite knowledge? Your guess is as good as mine: we can't.

Sadly, when you write against this "false-hearted" approach to literary fame, their penury-stricken legion of self-acclaimed Ogbanje boys and girls will squirm like hungry birds and accuse you of jealousy—probably on the grounds that Emezi has attracted great press, including making the cover of TIME magazine. But Akwaeke's approach is better understood by those who appreciate, from first-hand experience, that profiles of African writers—with very few exceptions—and the publicity that is garnered through those profiles cost these writers an arm and a leg, or sometimes their conscience. The objective is fame.

That they are now famous and presumably enjoy substantial material comfort cannot be argued, but one has to have limits in the pursuit of these comforts and one doesn't need to feel that they are in competition with someone else. That is a symptom of poverty that is not easily treated. Not even by wealth.

Predictably, when taking on a new client from the African literary class, western publicists come up with a theme to boost publicity for their client. The client would need to be onboard with the theme. The client can even suggest the theme but not everyone arrives at that point of reckoning with a readymade answer.

A nimble thinker, though, or one with keen opportunistic eye soonest finds their theme. It seems that in their case, Akwaeke chose Ogbanje as theme. I've been told that they got the inspiration to regard themselves as Ogbanje from Adichie herself! Apparently, it was Ms Adichie who told Akwaeke that they are Ogbanje. Emezi then thought to carve Ogbanje marks on their face.

"Women have two choices:
Either she's a feminist or a masochist."
- Gloria Steinem

A detour is necessary here. It seems fair to say that Ms. Adichie created the monster she must fight off now. I don't expect she will agree to my take. But it is undeniable that for good or evil, she is a powerful draw, including for a cast of characters driven to profit off her shine by demystifying her.

The whole spectacle leads me to indulge a subversive thought experiment: what could happen were Ms. Adichie a man? Predictable responses would range from accusations of bullying to insinuations of inappropriate sexual behaviour.

As that option is unavailable, a different form of slander has been deployed. As a friend said, if a man ever did what Adichie just did by writing the "It's Obscene" essay, people will call it bullying and insinuations of sexual relations will begin. It is unfortunate that the people she wrote about can be considered her family. But Ms Adichie needs to learn not to bring people who are not already successful close. People are desperate.

> *"Women are always saying,*
> *'We can do anything that men can do,'*
> *but men should be saying,*
> *'We can do anything that women can do.'""*
> - Gloria Steinem

In March last year, I was to travel to South Korea to interview the poet Ko Un. The old poet had his works removed from the curriculum in 2018 because of an allegation of sexual harassment. The younger generation of South Korean males began to fight back. They said they're being made villains of things the older generation did and they won't take it. The old poet was later found to be innocent. He had defended himself, saying in a statement that he had "done nothing which might bring shame on my wife or myself". He now lives with his wife in the south out of Seoul, a 30 minute-drive away from the popular city.

If we were to have only Akwaeke's account via their tweets about Ms Adichie, we would be tempted to join in the dastardly campaign to get Adichie cancelled. But we know now that someone has been using lies as a marketing strategy. Above all else, their Ogbanje claim shows they need medical help.

No human being in the history of the Igbo has demonstrated so much disrespect for Igbo cosmology as they have done.

It is a shame that when you write this truth about them and their claims, their fanboys and fangirls, most of whom are children who know nothing of Igbo culture, will say they have the right to be Ogbanje. No, you don't, you scoundrels! And you can't reference the Ogbanje narrative to any Western literature.

No! Akwaeke Emezi's account clearly differs from the established pattern of the Ogbanje in Igbo cosmology. In an interview with the BBC, Akuzzor Anozia, the Chief Priestess of Oguta Lake explained the concept of Ogbanje in clear terms:

"When a child is brought to us, we perform the rituals we have to, in the presence of her parents, to determine whether the child is Ogbanje or not. She goes further to say, "Sometimes, Ogbanje children come as Urashi, the God of Water. Ogbanje is Ogbuide, the Goddess of Water. Ogbuide (Ogbanje) was married to Urashi. She would disappear and appear. Why the rituals have to be performed also is to know whom the child reincarnated as. In Igbo culture, there is Life after Death. Everyone who dies returns as somebody else. *Nobody can wake up and give themselves mark that they are Ogbanje. It is done at childhood—when the child is a few months into the physical realm. Ogbanje is not a spirit*. It is a reincarnation of the River Goddess and they always come alone…You will know them from their childhood marks on the sides of their face."

I have italicized those parts above for emphasis. (You can listen to the full interview on BBC Igbo talking about it and the connection with Urashi).

It was only in 2017 as a grown adult that Akwaeke Emezi got the marks that now adorn their face and they gave themselves the marks as they themself had documented. They also did not "come alone". They have two siblings: a sister and a brother.

The case against Emezi's claim is clear. About Ogbanje, there is no question as to who to believe between the Chief Priestess of Oguta Lake, a globally renowned and revered custodian of Igbo spirituality, and the self-obsessed, self-deluded, publicity-hugging Akwaeke Emezi.

At the near-end of my documentary film, *The House of Nwapa*, the Chief Priestess of Oguta Lake deconstructs the concept of the ogbanje, comparing it to the concept of children born with dada. It will interest you that this documentary was screened at a film festival in Trinidad & Tobago in 2017, same place and year in which this Tamil writer locked themselves in a room and bruised themselves. In their words, they wrote: "Scar the child to discourage its return to the human world. Scar the child and it will no longer be ogbanje. (They are wrong, exposure does nothing to us.)."

This deluded person who needs to be checked into a mental home - apparently suffering from schizophrenia - has no respect for the Igbo belief system. They say, "They are wrong," yet, exploiting the roots of the religion and tradition. In African psychiatry, this person should have been locked up in a forest and whipped so the demons possessing them would disappear. It is also strange that the psychologists and psychiatrists (doctors) that they have seen in the US, couldn't diagnose them of a serious mental illness that has plagued them. Imagine telling yourself lies and believing the lies. Who intentionally uses a blade on their face, just to perfect a scam!

Akuzzor Anozia, in my film, *The House of Nwapa*, says: "You know Ogbuide does not choose the person who will serve her. It is destiny. According to my father, before I was born, he learned I will come into the world with a burden, not now that there are lots of churches. It was not like this back then. It was said that one month after I was born, a fowl should be killed to lift that burden off my shoulders. My father forgot everything he was told and I became ill. He went somewhere and was reminded what he was asked to do when I clocked one month. Then the fowl was brought and slaughtered to appease the gods and goddesses. Owing to the fact that whoever is serving Ogbuide will also serve other gods and goddesses, they appeased and begged the spirits. As a child, they took something and pasted it on my forehead. That was how I became well again."

What god or goddess in Igbo cosmology does Akwaeke worship that told them they are Ogbanje. This is not a situation where you are at will to decide if you want a sex change or not. Even that madness has its limits when it comes face to face with the Igbo belief system. You can't be selective of what you want in Igbo belief system. There is a pattern, and you either understand it in total or you don't. Our poor Akwaeke seems to have chosen where they stand—in the gut-churning mud of chicanery.

The social and political activist and feminist, Gloria Steinem, who is largely recognised as the face of the feminist movement in the sixties and seventies, said, a feminist is anyone who recognises the equality and full humanity of women and men. And I think that if anyone lies, whether man, woman or any other gender, they deserve to be told they are lying. This is not the same thing as attacking their sexuality,religion or gender; this is just telling the truth. They are liars. Akwaeke Emezi is a chronic liar who seems to believe their own lies.

Nigerian musician, Tkinzy, whose real name is Anthony Felix, only recently spoke about the marks on his face which he got as a child when he was very sick and his mother tried having more children. The children never came. His parents eventually died when he was very young. He was an only child to his parents and he has no sibling. There are other people I have spoken to, interacted with their parents. Their parents have not succeeded in having more children. The Ogbanje concept is not what people are proud to speak about publicly. A child who is known to be Ogbanje is feared. Definitely not Akwaeke.

Akwaeke didn't realize that an Ogbanje child gets their mark at birth! And that rituals must be performed by a Dibia. They didn't do proper research. They followed the fiction of Chinua Achebe in Things Fall Apart.

Akwaeke used razor and sat in front of a mirror in their room in Trinidad & Tobago and decided that they are Ogbanje and that the true source of this belief is wrong but either way, they must put some marks to complete the scam! What a thoughtless soul!

This madness must be stopped quickly before a seed of confusion on the nature of Igbo cosmology is planted for the next generation. This is why I keep meddling in this Adichie-Akwaeke-Ogbanje matter.

This would be the third time I am writing about them, and I will be writing more until they stop lying to sell books and achieve fame by deceiving people who believe their false narrative of the Ogbanje.

PART ONE

YOU CANNOT DECOLONIZE IMMIGRANT MENTALITY

Britain is an interesting place.

I will tell you why I said so in a bit, but I must warn that there is no shortcut nor straight road to the point I am trying to make. I have travelled to over 80 countries in the world. And in the European continent, I have seen half of the countries thereof. As an African making these trips with my Nigerian passport, you must assume it must have been hell for me. You guessed right; it gets really tough with all the racist, subtly confrontational, and over-the-top questioning at the passport control desk.

Not that such things have not happened to me in Africa, but you know, if an immigration officer in Johannesburg or Nairobi is being unnecessarily mean to me, I know it's not the colour of my skin. He is unlikely to suspect I am coming to overstay my welcome, or get married to their women and increase the local count of mixed babies. No, they do not think like this. They may simply be after some silly bribes, or it may be their pent-up Naijaphobia bubbling above the surface.

I had promised myself that this aspect of travel would never tame my love for constant mobility. I know my body; the flesh that encloses my soul. It cannot sit still nor bear being rooted to a spot for long. There is nothing I can do about the joy, the euphoric feel of my body in thermal ascent, cruising 38,000 feet above sea level with my favourite meal and book beside me. Very few things come close to the satisfaction that greets my face when the Ethiopian Air hostess, ever so graceful, asks if they can fill my cup with another round of cabaret. I drink to my fill knowing that a different war, another mind game awaits me at the border control desk.

Yes, I have had to swallow hard to keep my face warm to disarm petulant immigration officers. I have had to sound sarcastic sometimes to deflate the ones who ask three questions and expect a single answer. I have had to force a smile if I knew it'll save me one more minute of torturous standing and exit the interrogative burden of holding an African passport. These days, given my delicate mental health situation, I come to every immigration counter with all of my medication. All of them; although the Lithium Carbonate tends to stick out stubbornly in front. I think, or rather, I know that with my distinct sartorial taste, my walking stick (which has remained a close companion since I suffered a ghastly accident in 2018) and my transparent purse filled with medication tends to disarm the Gods of the gates of Europe. They are happy to quickly wave me into their paradise, but I know and I see the hordes of Africans who see *shege* from their hands. Turned back from heaven's gate to the hell they came from. And this is why I say Britain is an interesting place. Because unlike most places in Europe, the ones that turn you back look exactly like you; children of 'Multicultural Britain', who are more British than the British, are the watchers of the Empire. Very few countries, if any at all, understands the world much like Britain does. She understands emphatically the psychology of the dispossessed. The things immigrants and children of immigrants would do if presented with a veneer of representation; if given access, however pretentious, to the inner contours of the workings of society.

Britain, with its occasionally liberal immigration

laws have managed to welcome as many citizens of the new commonwealth nations as possible. They've also accorded them the privileges of citizenship and workplace representation that cannot be disputed. This is why, as I have come to notice, there are more ethnic minorities manning the immigration desk at London Heathrow Airport (LHR) today than anytime in history. However, the cost of Britain's generosity in this regard is felt by citizens of other commonwealth nations, especially if they are from Africa.

I do not know the stories of people arriving the United Kingdom from Asia or the Americas, but the ordeal of Africans in UK borders are known to me. I have heard and seen many stories. Some are in fact people close to me. It is not easy to pinpoint what is specifically at play for the border control officers, who feel a burning urge to manufacture the most ridiculous reason to deny an African traveller entry into Her Majesty's Kingdom. Of course, I am not trying to say that their Caucasian counterparts do not do the same. However, it does appear to me that because they have essentially been saddled with the responsibility of a distinguished gatekeeper in a place which they perceive as highly privileged, they go over and beyond to prove to the master that they are better gatekeepers of the holy gates of Britain; that as long as they are manning the ports of entry, Her Majesty's subjects can count on their callous ardency to sleep easy. That all being African or coming from an ethnic minority background, they are much more adept at uncovering the minds of their counterparts who were not as fortunate to have escaped earlier from the undesirable axis of the commonwealth map.

In the mix of this conundrum is a deep psycho-social failing that deserves to be thoroughly oxygenated. Though, I must admit that I have not sought to do so elaborately here. Still, it deserves to be said, and because I have seen it many times, immigrants from the not-so developed former colonies of Britain who migrate there and eventually become citizens tend to exhibit certain mentalities. For example, they tend to appeal to draconian immigration policies, some of which may have not turned out in their favour if they were yet to arrive Britain. In fact, a lot of Nigerians I know supported Brexit, and curiously so, because it was rarely for the same reason which the native British people did, but because they perceived that it made welcoming new immigrants much harder. In other words, the joy they tend to feel about their new status does not seem complete until they are able to convince themselves that they are part of a privileged minority who possess what their countrymen would find difficult, if not insurmountable to achieve. To stress this point further, any adult Nigerians would have seen tens or hundreds of videos on the internet in the last decades (many of them in the last three years since the hardship occasioned by the Buhari Administration triggered a sustained wave of exits to Europe, America and Canada) of Nigerians working in wintry conditions abroad. And with a phone in hand, the person goes on to make a video cautioning those back home about the horrible weather conditions which makes living abroad and settling abroad an onerous undertaking. They may also go on to say that those suffering the poor political and economic conditions back home are living easier lives because the standard of living is cheaper. Usually, this fallacy totally ignores the higher currency value and minimum wages being paid abroad for the most menial of jobs. The person behind the camera fails to mention the advantage they have over their countrymen in the areas of health interventions, basic freedoms, and of course a decent wage and living conditions. Their sole intention being to mask all the attractiveness of their Western abode, so that more of their countrymen won't join them. It is a perverse conceptualisation of the world, but this is real and people reason like this. I actually do believe that the Nigerian-British, Indian-British, Pakistani-

British or Jamaican-British immigration officers at the UK airports essentially imbibe this complex. Perhaps out of self-hate or Stockholm syndrome, they feel a need to easily criminalise the intentions of those who look like them. I cannot be sure, but I sometimes believe that they feel a sense of disdain for their own kind, standing on the other end of the wall now. They feel they belong to Britain now more than the place of their origin. Well, they have a right to feel that way, to bask in the light and privileges that Britain has given them. But this sense of loyalty to Britain should not place a veil over reason, over basic empathy, and over decency. What I have noticed is that these categories of citizens feel that what they owe Britain is to send back as many of their migrating countrymen as possible when they arrive at UK borders.

Was it what they were sent there to do? Do these positions come with a marching order which says, 'You know your people, now go make sure not one of them with a questionable motive or answer is allowed in.' This is what I call the immigrant mentality. It is all the pride the post-colonial subject enjoys from holding the passport and citizenship of a powerful nation even though those very privileges of citizenship remind him/her of the indignities they suffered in the country of their origin. From the foregoing, it would therefore seem that to retain the trust which was placed on them to deploy their talent and training in screening immigrants, they set about their day with a heart of stone. They do not always get it wrong, far from that. But they are also too quick sometimes, to bundle you home. I feel this way because they once set my friend packing. He was a young man in his early 20s whom had gone through the not so easy process of applying for his visa and paying for same. But at LHR, he trembled too much when the barrage of questions was thrown at him. He had no history of travel and so did not have the resources to calm himself and wriggle out of the tight corner the officers had pinned him. When you are afraid and consumed with tensions, even the most basic questions may elicit an unintelligible response. Sometimes, it is so bad that you could mispronounce the very words written in a paper and handed to you. So, at LHR, my young friend was not lucky. These officers, who would swear they were only doing their job, bundled him back home, and probably happy to be rid of one more 'economic migrant.'

They would not be the first to act in this way. Throughout humanity, people who feel less deserving of a privilege fight the hardest to deny same privilege to those who look like them. Like I had hinted earlier, this borders on a psycho-social failing which then produces in the mind of those who harbour it the idea that 'admitting too many of my own kind waters down the taste of the privileges this country has given me.' Do they see potential economic migrants who will come for the same opportunities as them in the future? Do they see potential migrants who will become permanent residents and UK Passport holders like them in future? Will too many passport holders from African states impact on their joy in being the few to share in the passport privileges that Britain confers? Of course, none of this should bother them, as the weight of a ship on water has no impact on the sea, so too, the value of whatever privilege they enjoy from Britain. Yet, one must not forget, as Achebe mentioned, the psychology of the dispossessed can be truly frightening. For the British government, it is a win-win. They have gotten the minority ethnic groups to stand at the city gates, profile and deport their own. For then, there would be no Caucasian face to this meanness, and Britain gets to say that they are truly a multicultural paradise.

CHAPTER ONE

PASSPORT IS A PAPER

Have you imagined or seen an Iroko tree without a stem that links its roots and branches?

The Iroko tree towers into the sky, bearing fruit and harboring birds of different species. But there is no stem. The absence of a stem is not because the tree is created or planted like that. It is not because of the nature of the specie. But circumstances displace the tree from its roots. This displacement serves as a harbinger of many challenges to the tree; it makes the progress of its branches and fruit-bearing retarded. It further creates room for uneven coordination of nutrient between the various branches and fruit-bearing.

As a teenager, the picturesqueness of an Iroko tree dominated my imaginations of Haiti; these thoughts were created by stories of how able-bodied young men and women were captured in the various villages and towns of Igboland during the obnoxious Trans-Atlantic Slave Trade and shipped to the New World where they were displaced from their roots. In those formative years, I learnt that during this era there existed what was called the Triangular Trade. One may ask: How did this trade work? Well, after the discovery of the Americas, the profitable plantation, and agriculture in the hemisphere, there was need for steady manpower to keep this profitable business afloat. Initially, the aboriginals, European objectionists and prisoners were ready source for the plantations. But they were not suitable for the work for certain reasons, including the lack of experience and resilience. Another source of labor was needed and Africa provided the solution to this problem. The Triangular Trade involved the business that revolved around the Mediterranean Sea. Here the European merchants traveled to Africa with such finished goods as tea and bayonets, which they exchanged with humans (slaves) who were then taken to the plantations in the New World. From the New World, they took home such raw materials as cotton and sugar. This singular activity led to the shipment of more than ten million Africans to the Western Hemisphere, of which the present-day Haiti was an integral part.

In the presence of the foregoing separations and the subsequent acculturation, something burnt in the minds of these slaves. These Africans felt severed from their roots without concessionary declamation; they felt they were made homeless through their wanton shipments to foreign lands; they felt they did not belong to the New World and, therefore, were nothing but orphans of Africa in an alien world where the oppressor was only interested in their labor and exploitation. They felt they were just African outcasts robbed of their dignity as humans and they had no hope of being of equal value before god and man. But they were humans, regardless of their victimized form. It was only their color that separated them from the others. While many of them accepted their place as bottom dogs in a Eurocentric world, others did not. The thirst to be free and equal grew higher. They expressed the desire through songs, poetry, and their music which revealed longing for their Paradise Lost in Africa, for an African Heaven where all Gods "chillun" have wings. They thought of Africa as one great country where all Africans would happily live together and free. They had a view of an Africa without a frontier or division. They envisaged a One United Africa. This idea made them to take bold steps towards freedom. They resorted to series of agitations and revolts. They aimed at building a nation in the style of what they thought of as an ideal African society. Among other series of activities, the Touissant Ouverture-led revolt of the 1791-1803 in Haiti was evident as it was instrumental in the independence of Haiti on 1st January, 1804 as Haiti became the first independent nation in Latin America and the only nation ever created as a result of a successful rebellion by slaves.

Haiti, Haiti, Haiti. How the country interests me. How I discuss her with several people, many of whom have called me a parrot (that I talk a lot) and a peacock (suggesting that my life is colorful, breezy and easy). I have never protested; this is more because of the way I travel. From one country to another, so I would focus on getting to Haiti by all means. I would travel as soon as possible to have a firsthand and direct encounter with the Haitians.

And in 2001, I was in Haiti. I was stunned to see that most of the images of the country was exactly what I had heard from friends. I left Havana to Port-au-Prince. I was coming from Cuba to Haiti. That was where I flew from, and I saw a lot of Cubans going to

Haiti and I wondered what was happening until we arrived there. It was a smooth immigration process. I'm not sure how much I paid. I think I paid $20 for visa on arrival and there was a stamp on my passport. The airport was small but coordinated. The Haitian people assumed I was Haitian and were speaking Creole to me. What I found most fascinating about it was that when I came out, I didn't see anything different from what I would see in Nigeria. It was the same behavior of people standing in front of the airport and waiting for their family members or friends who were returning or whomever they were picking. I was seated in a wheelchair because I needed special assistance.

So, there my driver was. He recognized me, came forward and took me, and while we were driving through the streets of Port-au-Prince, what I heard were Nigerian songs: Yemi Alade, Davido, and then the portholes, the dump sites, and gutters; they were like anything you could see in Lagos. To cut a long story short, the visual contortions of Haiti failed at nothing in emphasizing the conspicuous social multivalences which I was used to more than 8000 kilometers away in Lagos, Nigeria.

CHAPTER TWO

RACE IS NOT CREATED, NATIONALITY IS

What about the individual characters?

There are striking similarities between what was obtainable in Africa and Haiti. For instance, when I got to my hotel, there was a Haitian who was asked to take me around because he speaks English. I think he was deported from the US. He took that as a way of making a living, taking people around and explaining things to them, and I couldn't find any difference between him and the attitudes of people I know back in Nigeria. You know, like taking him to go eat, he would order food he knew he won't normally buy for himself because someone else was paying. This is an attitude that is common among young people back home, at least, the many who came around me at some point in my life. The similarities are too much. The only difference is the Creole and the French, Pidgin English and English Language, so it's a tad bit confusing to say these are not our people, nearly criminal even. I found the same energy and intensity in how the people behaved or acted in the open market. It was no different to the hurly-burly cast of markets that I have been to in south eastern Nigeria. The boisterousness of it all, the noise, the physical toil to get around packed bodies, the nearly belligerent bargaining, and, interestingly, the Haiti model of underhanded double-dealers could be seen lurking in corners and signaling unfortunate preys to devour. The stranded faces of those who were yet to get their sales numbers up or who may have not sold a thing on the day. The motorcycles trying to sneak through every little opening to convey their passengers, but the tricicyles and vehicles need to slip through the packed road markets too. It is organised bedlam, and a cacophony I instantly recognise. I have known it in Africa, and I can feel it here.

They are, folks, they are.

And they do things exactly like we do, and its stunning. I find that quite exhilarating. Nonetheless, when I began my real excursionist peregrinations, it became obvious that the general atmosphere is partly dreary, and in the main evocative of an unspoken longing for freedom from exanimate existence. Buildings are erect but lack spiritedness. Commercial activities are visible but lack the buoyancy of commerce. Street corners pockmarked with one extremity or another: drug peddlers, ever on pins and needles and chary of consequences, invent devious tactics for distribution of skunkweed and the likes. A handful of pedestrians, traversing the roads with lethargic motions; tradeswomen, vending wares with tapered indifference, recumbent on makeshift scrap boards or anything sufficient to pass as headrest; ambulatory hucksters, shambling towards whatever direction the wind blows the legs; pavements lined with unfettered debris, and so on.

The Haitians did not leave their African cultural practices behind as they traveled to the Western Hemisphere. As I mentioned earlier, one major thing I observed during my visit was the type of music they enjoy. One of the major places Nigerian music thrives in the western hemisphere is Haiti. The songs of such Nigerian musicians as Davido, Yemi Alade and so on punctuate the atmosphere of Haiti. As I have recognised the familiar feel and scent of home in the open markets and street corners of Haiti, it is follows that they too can recognise the familiar sounds of the motherland in the Afrobeats and other Afro-pop sounds.

From these expositions, one can discern that Haitians have been struggling to survive as individuals, groups and a nation, a hellish struggle about and against being Haitian. From 1804, when Haiti gained her independence, there have been pressures from both the international environment and otherwise. For instance, it was forced to pay France a massive indemnity for properties lost in those rebellions of the nineteenth century, and was ostracized socially and economically by countries all around the world. Haiti subsequently became entrapped in a cycle of poverty and misgovernment from which it has never emerged. Now, instead of being compensated for the many years of slavery, unpaid labor, dehumanization on slave plantations, encomienda systems, and so on by European nations, the country is plunged into the 120 years plus of debt payment to France and other countries, with 80% of Haitis GDP evaporating in the ungainful endeavor of debt servicing. Then, there is the financial burden hanging like the sword of Damocles over the head of the United Nations, during its cholera-diffusing peacekeeping mission-- though it later apologized to Haiti-- but it has failed to take financial responsibility. With all these, Haiti is the poorest country in the Western Hemisphere with more than 50% of the population living on less than US$1 per day. According to United Nations Human Development Index, Haiti ranks 145 out of 169 countries in the world. About 90% of her population does not have access to pipe borne water while more than 2/3 does not have access to electricity. This is a saddening economic condition. Coupled with an irregular and unstable government, the country was poorly planned. Buildings were poorly constructed in an ill-planed towns and villages of Haiti. This was to have a great effect on the country when the 12th January, 2010 earthquake happened. For instance, before the earthquake, while it was no seismic network in Haiti, there were very fewer seismologists who had to work with only one outdated and insufficient hazard map in the entire country. Furthermore, there was no earthquake preparedness program and no contingency plan for earthquakes. The typical university curriculum did not include seismic design, seismology, or the geosciences. These circumstances made it possible for the nation to be severely affected by the earthquake. The earthquake, which lasted for about 35 seconds to a minute, struck at approximately 25km south-west of Port-au-Prince, the capital city. It has been estimated that about 316,000 people died or missing, 300, 000 injured and over one million were rendered homeless. There was also massive damage in the metropolitan city which led to the destruction of government properties, private properties, NGO properties, United Nations properties, churches, and so on. Generally, the earthquake affected all the various groups of people in Haiti. Its nature was such that made it difficult for intervention programs to thrive on time. For instance, the country's airports were affected such that landing of planes became nearly impossible. Roads and other social amenities were also drastically affected in a way that interveners had to wait for days to devise strategies to assist the country.

One of the sectors that have traces of the horrendous earthquake was the educational sector. In the pre-earthquake days, emphasis on education in Haiti has been on improving the enrolment rate with an emphasis on girls; guaranteeing free compulsory education for all; integrating out-of-school children into education services; addressing violence in school; and the importance of developing a good national teacher training program. But the focus changed after the earthquake. This is because statistics showed that the earthquake happened in the heart of the town that carries more than 50% of the country's educational establishments. Consequently, a great number of the establishments were lost. For instance, about 1000 educational buildings collapsed, while more than 300,000 were rendered unusable because most of the structures were raised without considering seismic hazards. Therefore, it stands to argue that the educational planning went back to pre-21st century level. In her account, the Directorate of Plan Haiti summed that At 4:53pm on January 12, 2010, Plan staff had been in the country's head office in Port-au-Prince, concluding a major planning meeting. The mood was upbeat. For once, they had just been saying, the previous year had passed without any major crises neither hurricanes nor political instability and the team was planning to focus the next fiscal years strategy on doing more of what Plan had been doing best in Haiti for 37 years: long-term community development. Ten seconds later, everything was changed forever.

Eleven months after the quake, many schools are still operating under temporary structures that are vulnerable to hurricanes and heavy rains. Children are learning under tents that, with the combination of the bright sunshine and white canvas, create harsh lighting that strains their eyes and can cause headaches. Tents are also very difficult to ventilate and are therefore hot; this contributes to an uncomfortable learning environment.

One of the major cankerworms eating deep into the wheel of development in Haiti has been ill-politicking. This has been aided by politically sponsored gangsterism, thuggery and so on. Fortunately, the early years of the 21st century witnessed a commendable reduction in unstable government and political thuggery. This did not last for too long as the earthquake destroyed correctional centers and set loose some hardened criminals. According to the Haitian National Police (HNP), 5,136 prisoners escaped, including around 700 violent gang members. Some of these escapees have accessed hidden caches of weapons. As political tensions rise in the run-up to elections, armed groups, criminal enterprises and vulnerable young people could once again be mobilized by political forces to fuel violence or disrupt the political process. Gangs and their involvement in criminal and political violence are deeply rooted in Haitian politics, and fueled by widespread poverty, inadequate police presence, government weaknesses, and social and economic inequities.

Politically, history was made in the first election after the earthquake. For the first time in the history of Haiti, power was successfully handed over from a ruling party to an opposition party. Michel Martelly succeeded Rene Preval from May 14, 2011. With promises of massive post-earthquake reconstruction, the ovation and expectations were high. But, unfortunately, he also made many unpopular policies, one of which is the reinstatement of the military that had been banned by the past administrations. Michel was also accused of several corrupt practices. Before long, political and civil crises became prevalent in

Haiti as groups called for the president's resignation. By 25th October, 2015, presidential elections were held after a long period of delay by the incumbent; the result was controversial as it threw the nation into more turmoil. Series of crises, political and civil unrest forced Michel to resign on 10th February, 2016. This left Haiti without a president for one week. And on the 7th of February, Jovenel Moise became the president of the country after series of activities.

Without much ado, the same political turmoil that has punctuated the history of politics in Haiti did not allow Moise to complete his tenure as he was assassinated in his private home in Port au Prince on 7th July, 2021 by a group believed to be made up of 26 Columbians and 2 Haitian-Americans. Investigations have also shown that his assassination was politically motivated.

Eleven years ago, a seismic catastrophe compelled global attention towards Haiti, but this was short-lived as more natural, social, economic and political disasters have since befallen the nation.

The ruin of that catastrophe, however, bespeckles the evolutionary trajectory of Haiti. The human, material and atmospheric conditions of the nation seem to giveaway its yearnings for vivification.

There is a school of thought proselytizing the

exaction of reparation from European nations to Haiti. The argument here is bolstered by the many years of slavery, unpaid labor, dehumanization on slave plantations, encomienda systems, and so on by European nations. This argument is further bolstered by the over 120 years of debt payment to France and other countries, with 80% of Haitis GDP evaporating in the ungainful endeavor of debt servicing. Then, there is the financial burden hanging like the sword of Damocles over the head of the United Nations, during its cholera-diffusing peacekeeping mission--though it later apologized to Haiti-- but it has failed to take financial responsibility. The other school of thought, which is pragmatic, concerns the centralization of the human condition, the ultimate universal, as a propelling force in policymaking and the attainment of political consensus. An undertaking of sweeping political arbitraments, as a prelude to rapid socio-economic developments, cultural revitalization, and tangible improvement in the human condition, is urgently required. If pursued meticulously, such undertaking can alter the mode of Haitian transition from etiolation to rejuvenation.

Transition, as an agency of necessity and continuity, can either facilitate transformation or precipitate deterioration. As an agency of political necessity, transition sub-serves the real and the abstract, melding together the will of the collective and the force of constancy. It engenders political justice through inclusive participation and dilates the boundaries of accomplishments through eclecticism. If deprived of heterogeneity, however, it becomes caustic, vitiated by unfettered ambitions and subhuman calculations. Transition is also a process of acknowledging the faults of the present and a relentless commitment to a future of transformative excellence.

When I got approved to volunteer at Queensland University in Haiti by the administration of the Queensland University through Dr. Jean Claude, I was very excited about going to Haiti because it had always been my dream to go to Haiti.

Reading about President Duvalier and his sort of interest in Igbo people through the Biafra struggle: he went to the United Nation defend the Biafra struggle and ask the United Nation to intervene in the massacre of the Igbo people, and he addressed the Igbo people as his own people. It was interesting to find that information. I began to read things on Haiti and found out about Christopher who was the first monarch of Haiti and he was a descendant of the Igbo people.

CHAPTER THREE

SLAVERY WAS NEVER ABOLISHED

"40 million people are estimated to be trapped
in modern slavery worldwide."
(Anti-slavery)

To hell with abolitionism! That may come across as
harsh, but it's the truth! Did some of the European
and American powers that spearheaded the anti-

slavery drive in the 18th century succeed? "Under the leadership of William Wilberforce and Thomas Clarkson, these forces succeeded in getting the slave trade to the British colonies abolished in 1807. The United States prohibited the importation of slaves that same year, though widespread smuggling continued until about 1862."(Encyclopedia Britannica) I'm not trying to discredit the efforts of abolitionists. For example, men like William Lloyd Garrison, the founder of the American Anti-Slavery Society, who denounced slavery and even faulted the American constitution for accommodating slavery. I must commend his like mind for their indefatigable efforts, but that does not mean that I agree that their mission was successful. That people are not carted in chains in their numbers on a ship doesn't mean that there is no slavery going on in our modern world. I choose to say that there is what I see as neo-slavery, which is systematic in our present day. "But right now, millions of children and adults are trapped in slavery in every single country in the world." (Anti-slavery). I'm vividly convinced that many who are under this modern chain may be freed after this liberal piece of mine.

Some of you have already concluded that I will be writing about human trafficking, as it is the most common slavery in our contemporary world. I don't have any concern about that now. That does not mean that I'm in support of human trafficking, but I want to draw your attention to areas we neglect or may have seen in our contemporary society, of which many are victims, even the so-called educated elite, but they may not know it is slavery.

I'm saddened to say that some African countries' identities are dashing into extinction as a result of acculturation. It beats my imagination that English and French are still the official languages in most colonized countries of the world, especially in African countries where indigenous languages abound in their thousands. That the African continent, with the exception of Ethiopia, was colonized doesn't mean that we should continue to hold onto the languages of our colonial masters. I know that countries like China were colonized by Britain and Germany, but today, their official language and language of instruction in their schools has been Mandarin. The same is applicable to India colonized by Britain, but their official language, even in school, has been Hindi in Devanagari script (Article 343 of the Constitution). It pains me that in Nigeria and most African countries today, English, French, or any other foreign language are their official languages, even in schools, to the

extent that children are whipped for speaking their
indigenous languages, aka vernacular, in classes. It
pains me more that indigenous languages, especially in
Nigeria, are no longer core subjects in schools. Those
who opt for external examinations such as WASSC
or NECO do so with levity, knowing that failure will
not affect their performance in the exam. You will be
surprised to see that out of nine subjects students sit
in an exam, a child may score highly in eight, but a
failure in the English Language, even with a passing
mark, will be a total wastage to the entire examination
or result. But if one fails in an indigenous language
like Igbo, Hausa, or Yoruba, so long as the English
language is good, there is still hope for that child. This
slavery must stop!

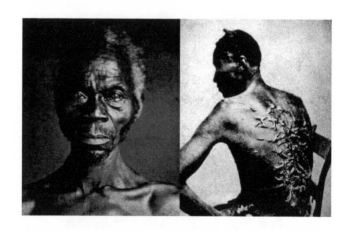

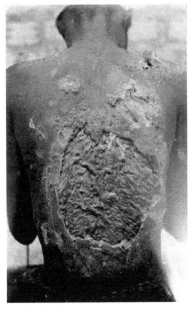

Recently, most Nigerian schools are abandoning the Nigerian curriculum to teach the British or American curriculum. How can a child in Nigeria learn the curriculum designed to cater for the needs of British children in Nigeria? As if that is not enough, we enroll our children in the IGCSE examination, which is at a cutthroat price. An attempt made to undermine the African-based examinations even when they are richer in content. I must tell you, on a yearly basis, millions are carted away from the shores of developing nations because of this examination. The most annoying thing is the Cambridge Primary and Lower Secondary Checkpoint examinations, which have no value even in the host country of the examination body. Despite this fact, African parents are meant to spend a fortune registering their wards for this examination or purchasing the books. "Checkpoint is not a formal qualification with a certificate, although students get a Statement of Achievement." (Catalyze, 2018). This foreign curriculum and examination slavery must stop!

A friend once narrated to me his ordeal some years back, what happened during one of his interviews, which after that made him relocate to a foreign country. He said that after the interview, there were two people that reached the final stage. He was shocked when human resources personnel told him that the company would have taken him but because he had his masters' degree in Nigeria and the other guy had his own in one foreign country which I cannot mention here. Taking him would be an advantage to the company. This is how he was discharged from a job he had merited. This singular reason made him leave the shores of Africa to get a foreign degree, even if it was only a diploma. Go to big institutions in Nigeria or Africa. They prefer foreign expatriates to home-based professionals. What breaks my heart is that most of these expatriates who are paid in pounds and dollars do nothing or little when the home-based professionals do much of the work and receive little in local currencies.

"........expatriate employment is morally wrong because it perpetuates external domination and control.... the enormous pay disparity between expatriates and local professionals. It has been noted that, although expatriates work shoulder to shoulder with similarly qualified local professionals (Welch 2003), expatriate salaries are usually considerably higher than those of local professionals. In some cases, this disparity could mean that expatriates earn as much as 20 to 50 times the salary of local professionals. In fact, in many cases, the housing allowance of an expatriate is higher than the salary of a local employee of similar rank." **(Okeja Uchenna, pg 65-67, 2017)**

I'm really interested to know what it means by 'United States-Africa summit,' 'the Africa-China summit,' 'Tokyo International Conference on African Development Summit,' 'Russian-African Summit,' etc. Don't you think that is underestimating for a country to wake up from her sleep just to summon the leaders of African continent – the world's second-largest and second-most populous continent of 54 countries to discuss the development of the continent? This is disgusting! It doesn't matter how anyone else wishes to see this; I see it as a hubristic devaluation of autonomous statuses. They wake up and summon African leaders at their own convenience and condition them on how they will run their continent. They have finally succeeded in turning them to beggars and determine almost everything that happens in the politics, economy, etc of the continent. Two of the greatest weapons of slavery on African leaders are Foreign aids and loans. Those foreign aids and loans have no impact rather done more harm than good to the continent. The present-day African leaders are gradually giving out the African continent and her future to slavery without them knowing it. African leaders need to break this chain!

"Giving alms to Africa remains one of the biggest ideas of our time—millions march for it, governments are judged by it, celebrities proselytize the need for it. Calls for more aid to Africa are growing louder, with advocates pushing for doubling the roughly $50 billion of international assistance that already goes to Africa each year. Yet evidence overwhelmingly demonstrates that aid to Africa has made the poor poorer, and the growth slower. The insidious aid culture has left African countries more debt-laden, more inflation-prone, and more unattractive to higher-quality investment. It's

increased the risk of civil conflict and unrest (the fact that over 60% of sub-Saharan Africa's population is under the age of 24 with few economic prospects is a cause for worry). Aid is an unmitigated political, economic and o disaster." – (**Moyo Dambisa, 2009**)

Furthermore, who would believe that despite the slogan of Pan-Africanism, 'Africa for Africans,' that Africans would have the mind to subject fellow Africans to slavery? It is a common knowledge that there are several forms of slavery going on in Africa created by Africans. A typical example is the slavery business in Libya. "Slavery is thriving in Libya, where thousands of black Africans hoping to get to Europe instead find themselves bought and sold, forced to work for nothing, and facing torture at the hands of their owners." (Mark Monica, 2018). Another example that drains me because I had firsthand information from a friend is working without retirement plan. How do you feel as a capitalist that somebody will give his 25 years in your firm and came out empty-handed? This friend told me that he worked in a big private firm for seven years and resigned because he saw that he has no future there. These groups of CEOs will not give you employment letter, they want you to kill yourself while working under harsh conditions for them and at the end of the month, they will either owe you or deduct your money because of one grievous rules and regulations they set out just to steal their workers slavery. "Modern slavery is the severe exploitation of other people for personal or commercial gain. Modern slavery is all around us, but often just out of sight. People can become entrapped making our clothes, serving our food, picking our crops, working in factories, or working in houses as cooks, cleaners or nannies." (Anti-slavery). Some of them will go to the extent that they are collecting your tax from the little salary only for them to pocket it without remitting to the appropriate government agency. It is time for government of developing countries to sit up and look into the staff welfare of most of these private-owned institutions. People are passing a lot of hell under them.

Lastly, let me say this: I'm always annoyed when Africans are called BLACKS but the one that annoys me most is when I see African elite call themselves Blacks or accept that title when it is used to address them. African intellectuals do not see anything wrong in being colourised as Black! "The terms 'black' and 'negro' were coined to dehumanize people from the African continent to serve the imperialist and colonial agendas of Europe and the US... For me, "black" and "negro" are two sides of the same coin. They are inherently derogatory labels – imposed on Africans to discredit their humanity and to boost a false sense of white superiority. There is no other way around it. And whichever way you look at it, to continue to call us by labels we were called in plantations and its after-party is at the very least immoral – if not racist, unexamined as it might be." (Vava Tampa, 2019). When you are referred to as a Blackman it simply means you are an Ape. Those who are familiar with the words of slave masters or colonial masters to their African slaves when they want to order them to do something would not see 'Apes obey!' slogan as a new thing. It is the collective tranquilization of the sensibilities of Africans home and abroad which makes this calculated monstrosity largely ignored. When you are referred to as black, it means that you accept to be an evil person because those who coined such inhuman term tagged almost everything related or connected with black evil. The vehicle used to convey prisoners is called Black-maria, the devil is black, blackmail, blacklist, etc. This nonsense must stop!

CHAPTER FOUR

THE ISSUES WITH GLOBALIZATION

"Globalization is not only something that will concern and threaten us in the future, but something that is taking place in the present and to which we must first open our eyes."
– Bill Gates, owner and former CEO of Microsoft

I'm not sure what comes to mind when you hear the word "globalization." Do you believe it when someone claims to have eaten lunch on the moon or the sun? At the very least, Neil Armstrong, Edwin "Buzz" Aldrin, and Charles "Pete" Conrad are known to have been among the first twelve humans to walk on the Moon. Tell me of someone who has successfully walked on the sun. There is no one. A 17-year-old Korean was the first person to walk on the sun, according to a North Korean Central News broadcast from 2014. This report is still widely regarded as a fantastic today.

You don't need to be reminded that enduring the sun's rays despite being 93 million miles away, let alone getting closer to it, takes a lot of guts. Globalization is like a man who claims to have eaten his lunch outside in the sun. It is, in fact, a myth. The world would have been a better place by now if globalization was genuinely as real as most people think. However, globalization is nothing more than socio-cultural, economic, intellectual and political ideology used by international powers against weak countries in order to further their own self-aggrandizing objectives.

"Globalization operates mostly in the interests of the richest countries, which continue to dominate world trade at the expense of developing countries..."
– (BBC)

We live in a globalized world, and China is busy dominating African markets with its businesses and industries, even when great businesses and industries are not owned by Africans in their country, where the government is constantly introducing new measures to bludgeon privately-owned companies and businesses. Olson Stephen (2020) stated clearly in his work, "China has often been criticized for a lack of transparency, especially with regard to its economic and trade policies. While in many cases, these criticisms are valid, they belie the fact that, in other instances, China is remarkably open and transparent about its intentions and ambitions (The Diplomat)." So when the so-called experts define globalization as the free movement of people and goods and cultures from one country to the other, it is important to pause and ask, whose goods, whose persons, and whose cultures? The evidence before our eyes suggests that is the goods of the rich people that travel from their domains and end up in African markets or those of poorer countries. It is their cultures that travels and get consumed in weaker countries, so that in time, they become dominant. It is the people of the richer countries who get to travel, thanks to injustice and inequities of passport hierarchies. It is true that the poorer countries of the world have not exactly helped themselves due to poor leadership whom they either elect or whom are foisted on them. Corrupt government officials, even in my own village in Nigeria provide access to rapacious

Chinese plunders. They mine the resources of the local people with reckless abandon. They engage in vicious deforestation, mowing down the mahogany trees which had enriched our ecosystem. They move around with security forces whom the authorities pawn over to them, having first impoverished them with abysmal wages. The Chinese have not been all bad news nonetheless. They at least, attempt to offer loans to African governments, even though the later often use it to feather their own nest. When these loans are tied to infrastructure however, the Chinese will arrive to build it with a labour force from China, drawn from Chinese prisons and kitted with their concealed ankle-monitors. One sees therefore that globalisation merely opened the gates for already-powerful nations to prey on the developing ones even more spectacularly.

It is equally critical to highlight that the United States of America is not immune to this truth. "Globalization is seen as Western imperialism as well as Americanization. For instance, globalization encourages people to buy American goods and services, which ultimately undermine deep-rooted communal values." (Golebiewski Daniel, 2014)

"The consequences of globalization are far from homogeneous: income inequalities, disproportional wealth and trades that benefit parties differently. In the end, one of the criticisms is that some actors (countries, companies, individuals) benefit more from the phenomena of globalization, while others are sometimes perceived as the "losers" of globalization. As a matter of fact, a recent report from Oxfam says that 82% of the world's generated wealth goes to 1% of the population." (Youmatter, October, 2020)

As earlier noted, the African continent has become a dumping ground for European and Asian countries as a result of globalization. Everything so far has been sellable due to the fact that it is Africa. And they've succeeded in instilling in the minds of many Africans the belief that anything that isn't foreign is inferior. The more they preach their globalist agenda, the more powerful and influential they get, and the less powerful and influential the recipients become. "Globalization has increased inequality in developing nations between the rich and the poor. The benefits of globalization are not universal. Globalization is making the rich richer and the poor poorer (Xenia Madelin Bonilla, 2016)."

Unfortunately, it is general knowledge in Africa that there is a dearth of health practitioners, particularly in Nigeria, the world's most populous African country. The World Health Organization (WHO) advises one doctor for every 600 patients and a critical threshold of 23 doctors, nurses, and midwives per 10,000 patients, while in Nigeria, there are four doctors for every 10,000 patients and 16.1 nurses and midwives. Despite this, the world's rich countries, which claim to genuinely care about the developing world, continue to court health professionals with their dollars and pounds. The same can be said for other areas of the economy. I'm not sure what will happen to the unfortunate masses if they succeed in capturing all of the best minds and hands, particularly from the African continent. I understand that people will readily migrate to where their labour is priced better, and places they feel their lives would be more secure. This consideration continues to pull professionals in Africa and drive them to the West. It is an indictment on African governments but even those are tone deaf and impervious to reason. I have also noticed that Western countries want these things for Africa, draconian leaderships that bound its peoples to the chains of oppression. That shrinks the civic space and threaten and kill protesters. The relationship between France and their former colonies is a glaring evidence of this. The British interference in Nigeria's political leadership, their clear and unashamed preference for the Fulani to misrule Nigeria is well-known. Leaders who are politically conscious are often subtly-threatened or sabotaged to fail.

Unfortunately, most Africans today will not be brave enough to talk about or be proud of their culture. Tell me how many young Africans can tell us about the Omenala of their ancestral regions or forefathers while globalization claims that Africans have no knowledge of God and that our predecessors were pagans who had no close relationship with God and thus were condemned to hellfire. We now have a new religion as a result of globalization, which we embrace even in this modern world. Even those who married us into this religion are amazed at how the average African man practices his religion nowadays. Have you observed that the African value system is in jeopardy of being extinct? Who is to blame for this? I recall that children in the past enjoyed akuko ifo – these rich folktales were the guiding principles that shaped African children's strong moral value. What happened to the moral value of African children today? It is extremely concerning that a significant portion of our teeming adolescents are now involved in narcotics, cultism, prostitution, computer fraud, and a variety of other vices that sting anyone who hears about them. It was recently discovered that young Nigerians are becoming hooked to methamphetamine, or crystal meth, also known as mkpurummiri among the Igbo people of the South East, and that it was smuggled by international drug traffickers.

More tragically is how our culinary choices have now been dramatically altered. The organic food which our fore-fathers ate and remained mostly of sound health is now a thing of the past. We enthusiastically consume all kinds of canned and chemically modified food. Those who can afford the most processed food believe they are well-to-do, and those who cannot feel that they've been left behind. Africans are now like a people sitting behind a wall of ignorance erected for them by their enemies. We do not consume the alcoholic beverages of our fathers, which is *nkwu-enu*, but sundry whiskey brands imported from the West. We consume beer in such enormous quantity, while many do not care to know if their anatomy is compatible with barley or not. Fresh palm wine is consumed these days at special events and December festivities. Those who would tap it and ready it for consumption are dwindling in numbers. And because we abandoned it as a beverage of choice, its entire supply chain has suffered. What you abandon cannot grow nor expand. Certainly not at the same rate with other competitive products. Fewer people know how to tap palmwine today more than ever. Not that people should still undertake what can sometimes be a dangerous sojourn up the tree, but the lack of consumption interest in the beverage also foreclosed all the innovation that it could bring about. There is no reason why Africans or the Igbo people could not have manufactured a machine that goes up the palm tree and taps palmwine. So, here, we can easily deduce and discern the tragedy of colonial mentality, where all that is local is inferior even if it saves us, and all that is foreign is superior even if it kills us.

"Globalization has led to the spread of western culture and influence at the expense of local culture in developing countries like Africa. Most people now in developing countries cop what people in developed countries do. So, it's like they ignore their own culture and practice western culture." (UK Essays, July, 2021).

It's time for Africans to exercise your common sense! It is past time to correct the record and inform every living soul on the planet that wicked activities do not originate in Africa. The majority of them were globalization's gifts. Amadioha, our Chi, is widely regarded as a god of justice and wrath. In the past, he always struck anyone who engaged in evil activities. People were aware of this and avoided doing wrong in order to avoid Amadioha's anger. Today, brothers commit suicide, clerics sleep with married women on the pulpit, and nothing happens that could never happen under the watchful eye of Amadioha. Ala ga akugbu onye ahu! In a sense, globalization continues from where colonialism stopped in the muddling of how Africans understand themselves, spiritually. Colonialism pulled Africans from their practice disparate religions to one of religious homogeneity, where people are either boxed into Christianity or Islam. Traditional religious worshippers who do not conform to either modes of worship are then stigmatized, so that those who feel alienated would attempt hold on to both for acceptance. With the advent of globalization and different countries willing to export or support different agendas abroad, religion has become a tool for to control and influence things in other countries. I have read about humongous funding being provided to parts of northern Nigeria for the promotion of sharia beliefs. Christians believe it is normal to imagine those who do not worship their God to be destined for hell. Overzealous ones among them have gone to the extent of burning down harmless shrines where traditional priests or worshipers offer their own supplications. The stories created by our writers, the films created by our filmmakers have also, contributed to these unsavory happenings. Africans have internalised the untrue and sometimes hateful narratives of the West towards them, and gone on to reproduce these lies about themselves. Yet, it is also Africans who pay for social, economic and political disasters that arises in their societies as a result of globalization.

Today's world is more insecure as a result of globalization. Terrorism is becoming more prevalent over the world. Many terrorists enter a foreign nation on a visa with the intent of carrying out a terrorist act. It's a situation that diminishes the obligation of good neighborship in society. Terrorists, however, convince young people and inhabitants of the country that they are doing the right thing. That's why there is fear, mistrust, and tension in society. For example, the Nigerian government has been battling Boko Haram terrorist organization for nearly twenty years with no success. The government has declared on multiple occasions on major news sites that they have defeated them technically, but this organization has continued to go on the rampage and perpetrate horrific crimes against humanity. And no one would believe that their sturdy pillars are external, powerful subsurface hands. Who supplies the terrorists with all of those strong bullets? Globalization is a 21st-century monster.

Who hasn't noticed that mortality rate is high? Is it connected to globalization in any way? Yes! Globalization has caused many indigenous people to forget and discard the majority of their natural foods, which they were given by God. Globalization has resulted in the use of processed foods and the use of pesticides in crop growing to reduce the length of growth and boost profit. Animals such as cows are fed chemicals to make them produce a lot of milk or gain weight for those sold to the meat industry in order to benefit from business. Chronic diseases are on the rise as a result of increased chemical consumption from meals, resulting in a high mortality rate. Unfortunately, no concrete steps have been deployed to address the environmental contamination caused by most of the world's largest multinational corporations in developing countries. It is commonly known that the lives of the people of Nigeria's Niger Delta region have been jeopardized since the discovery of oil there.

"Communities in the Niger Delta know first-hand, both the devastating impacts of the climate crisis and how extractive companies like Shell put their profits before people, leaving behind a trail of entrenched poverty, pollution, destruction and rights abuses." (ActionAid International)

Despite the Paris Agreement's goal of limiting global warming to 1.5 degrees Celsius by decreasing CO2 emissions by 45 percent by 2030, firms like Shell find it difficult to align their business models to it. "Shell has known that drilling for oil and gas causes climate change for decades and is among just 100 fossil fuel producers responsible for 71% of the harmful greenhouse gas emissions causing global warming since 1988." (ActionAid International). It's all thanks to globalization, which opened the gateway for them. Globalization, according to the majority of myopic people, has aided in the reduction of unemployment rates in developing countries. None of them bother to conduct their own independent investigations to determine whether these foreign-based countries are providing adequate care for their employees. According to the IndustriALL global union, contract workers in Shell, Nigeria, who work even longer hours than permanent employees, are underpaid or not paid on time.

IndustriALL Global Union interviewed a community contract worker who had the following grievances:

"My contractor doesn't pay when due. I haven't been paid for six months. My salary is just 50,000 naira (US$137) a month. I will go home and beg my neighbour for food. For six months my children can't go to school. I've been working for eleven years at Shell but I don't have carpet in my house. I don't have a radio in my house.

"If you open your mouth and you want to say something, they will sack you. The next day they (Shell) will call that contractor and they will sack you and they will bring in another person. That's what we're facing at this particular Shell (operation)."

The aforementioned and many more examples show how, as a result of globalization, indigenous peoples in developing countries endure rowdy treatment from foreign-based enterprises in their territory, despite the fact that we know such unimaginable treatment cannot be extended to their citizens. Globalization is a 21st century fraud!

I don't even know how to talk about the immigration vacuum created by developed countries in the world. Again, if, according to the Peterson Institute for International Economics, "Globalization is... flows of investment, people and information," why is it so difficult for people from developing countries to get into developed countries in the world? We hear about illegal migration, but nobody is interested in digging out the roots behind it. Will people migrate to these countries illegally if immigration processes are flexible in these developed countries? I must tell you that most of the people who try to get into these developed countries are those who are frustrated with the rigorous processes of getting there legally. Sometimes people will spend a lot of money to get a visa only to be turned down at the last minute.

Globalization is a foreign term, and it is important that the developing countries understand that it is not in their interest or meant in any way to favour them. Thus, they should work hard to create another term that would work for them until the developed countries of the world are ready for true globalization. "He **Who Comes Into Equity Must Come With Clean Hands.**"

CHAPTER FIVE

THE SIGNIFICANCE OF DECOLONIZATION

Is Racism an invention?

Very much, Yes. A colonial, imperial edict that now is synonymous with several African-renaissance terminologies: black, for example, which not only psychologically conditions the intended group of people but also regularizes their socio-economic behaviors, aspirations, and political inclusions. Adelaide's Mista Courifier1 is an important literature that climaxes the 'African-' dilemma. Mr. Courifier, in the novel, represents a psychology-complex material for White supramacism, whose strife for White-validation was thematic, enough, and his son's, Tomas, rebellion against domination represents, for instance, Perpetual Colonial subjugation and Resistance. Thus, Decolonization is made important and family, 'percursor… of a social group or nation,' is the simplest experiment-form, in testing what shape the Society is.

Brazza's diary is an important divergence point to begin with:

> *Brazza: White men have two hands. The stronger hand is the hand of war. The other hand is the hand of trade. Which hand do the Abanhos want?*
> *Abanhos (all together): Trade*
> *From Brazza's diary, September 1881[2]*

Brazza's diary depicts the tragedy of pre-Africa, and what Africa remains after Rhodesia became Zimbabwe in late nineteenth century, after 'God Save The Queen' was sung. By the time, Black, rightly said by Lfroi Jones, was a Country, a dump-ground for Colonial predecessors, for used everything: clothes, cars, ideas, and second and third-class academic system. Newly-born 'Black' countries, then, had one role of institutionalizing into the White system: a suit at all times, with a spectacle, feet clad in socks... It became honorable to look like the Colonizer, even more honorable till today to have academic certifications there—the latter, I must say is a boomerang of monkey-dey-follow maxim, which pivotal African leaders have allowed for foreign investors. Foreign investments in Africa became a political propaganda; illicit gold-digging in DRC continues; oil rigs in the Niger Delta area caused countless casualties. Other places may have been subtler, especially in the acquisition of classroom knowledge. The African is considered less, their teachers, if not underpaid, are shackled by the curricula. The African is taught the history of Slavery. That, because, the Colonial institution made slavery an epicenter of Africa; and the aboriginal cultures this African learns whilst growing up is debased, even criminalized. The surviving cultures are those that embrace westernism, that doesn't pose a threat to the continuous canonization of Europeocentrism. This, invariably, is made possible through visual sensations; the Europeocentric says, "it is obscene that Africans enslave women." The cretin nods, though he's African, he has no brains. And doesn't ask if community in Africa was a slave ship from Portugal or Great Britain; and this cretin refuses to ask why femininity seemed to only reincarnate with the advent of Colonial machinery since the mid 1800s; and this cretin, this African, who goes about saying feminism is a 'western thing' that 'womanism' is an 'African thing,' this same cretin, an African, who distinguishes feminism from womanism as one which empowers women too much that they incapacitate the man. This is the same cretin that watches a Whitism-dominated film—that colorizes a lie to augment moral sensation on femininity, politicism, socio-economies, a perfect White World where girls grow happy, simple, where men acts liberally— and this same gets home, sees their 'black' family, and sees this 'black' father beating this 'black' mother and he concludes, ostensively, that marital strife and women-hating, and mansplaining is an African thing. And anything else, and better, is a White thing.

As children in Nigeria, two things were irrepressible in us: the love for cinema, and our inhibition with the academics—the serious, then, who are enamored of the gnosis of learning and academic activities, engage exclusively in 'cerebral activity and not an emotional felt experience.' [3]

The enjoyable of them makes do with the foundational stereotypes: the black Indian, or the African, acts as the foil or the antagonist, the terrorizing ogre. Whilst it was hard to imagine a wicked fair-skinned, we saw them as superior somewhat, or as friends, or as prospective colleagues but never ever as inferiors. So, the tangle here for the African child is in dichotomy: one, the cerebral ingestion of what 'Is'— that is, the simulacrum of the White superiority—and what 'Ought'—reality of Africa's place in history, at the nadir of humanity, the black, the debased, apparently the Satan. Inadvertently, these films have eroded the autochthonous culture that elicits self-esteem, and have made the foreign propaganda of perpetual African economic enslaving the 'Is' and 'Ought' of socio-interrelation. Thus, a hostile environment is one which the 'White' is present, where the 'Black,' no matter their religious, cultural, political, moral inclinations, becomes neighbors. 'Black' neighborhoodness in White communities has then become a wall the March on Washington cannot destroy.

Second, shallow esteem for cultural representations sets in. For example, the Oduduwa (in Yoruba), the Ala (in Igbo), the Orixas (in Brazil), and other several Gods are referred to, alphabetically as 'gods,' to project differences, and, in strict Celestial practices, they become Satanic or apostatical— whether Gods of mischief, of Wealth (as in, the Senteria, androgynous Olokun), or of Harmony, or of creativity, etc. A culture of erosion reinforced by Christainity.

Whether these 'satanic' practices were cultural or religious have little essence when the hooves of Imperialist deconstruction set in. As is apparent, being a Catholic, a Protestant, a Cherubim, etc., were the options—the Ideal 'good' on the path to 'eternal rest' and the wearing of beads, of anklets, of bracelets, were seen, ultimately as the worship of devil. Adornment of beads is a less subject matter to the controversies of tattooing in the Celestial context, as 'adultery,' too. In pre-Colonial Oyo empire (in Nigeria), Yoruba parents tattoo their children with the Children's name or the name of their compound, in case these Children got lost. Or they mark their cheeks, for beatification. That culture, now, has gone under because it looks barbaric. Whether it went under because of its 'barbarity' is not the argument, except that especially women with cicatrices are seen as scarred, less complete, or a victim. Can one be a victim of their culture? The full-lip, too, has its own fair share of racial redistribution; the full-lip, even though was a major body feature in old Egypt,

(Kemet), it also has gone under, and no lips, or small lips, and pink, are now the ideal body types. The same as women's legs, which are supposed to be skinny to look chic. Though there'd been deliberations on the ideal masculine body, whether muscled, or skinny, one thing remains certain whatever, that it'd be communicated soon.

(Nike's Gallery, Lagos and elsewhere, plays an important, rebel role in pre-discussed idealism, with the Gele, which I shall not translate, with fashion, the African way.)

Hyperrealiism, and Hume's analysis on 'Is' and 'Ought' shall be discussed, here, in reference to my being acclimatized to rebellion of the modern Colonial institution. Hyperrealism means a doctored reality. Hume's analysis on 'Is' and 'Ought' infers that no validating connection between Induction and Deductive Reasoning exists, that is, 'no connections between factual statements and moral judgment.'[4]

In Context, hyperreality—or a simulacrum! — has been by far the major-wielding tool of colonization which is not limited to canonization of 'Black literatures' and the celebration of Black History Month alone. (What does Black History Month mean, anyway, if it isn't fetishizing the very colonial institution?) Blackness creates a mirage for the

African, or even the less/none African (the Latino, the half Chinese, the Mulatto, for example); Blackness connotes its immediate opposite. The question remains whose skin is White, and whose is Black?

Hyperrealism has revolved, around so many of us, about these terms: what does structuralism and post-structuralism mean for Africans? Why have racist slurs become prominent, even in basic settings? Why have the non-African been put in a reactionary position—by simulating their sensual, insecure tendencies of the thick-skinned? Why has the technicality of colonial, linguistic units not changed, though the majority of African languages have wound up in the dictionary of regional varieties of English? Hume's 'Is' and 'Ought' surfaces; the urgency of post-structuralist studies follows thus; the reconstruction of Hollywood stereotypes, too, or the pulling down of it—whose stereotypes I find appalling, especially when characterizations are predictable—where the Black has to grapple with racism, and it has to do *always* with anger management issues— because it's hedonistic to buy what fuels the status quo than what rebuilds it: an example is the role of thick-skinned Indians in Bollywood, why African-American actors still are slurred…

To say things as they are is historicism, to construct

things as they should be is, in part, Art. Art can play a functional part in curbing stereotypes of Black-White-Colored color bar; Literatures doesn't have to be Black; Prizes doesn't have to be Black; a Continent doesn't have to be Black; an entire continent can stop being *planet of the apes*; there shouldn't be the Black American, the Black British, the Non-natives black. For me—and for Africans' else—to stay in a segregated community provides comfort than to stay in other 'White' communities. I'd feel safe when the Media talks about a 'Black' violence, than one Joshua, who is black, who murdered his former School teacher in Wisconsin, who is White; it feels safe because one 'Black' man understands his fellow 'black' man—in a survey by Unite Students, a student accommodation provider in the UK, the Guardian reports,[5] "Three-quarters of Black students reported an impact on their mental health due to racism, compounded by a lack of support and difficulties in finding Black counsellors who had the experience to understand the impact," though it is imperative to know that over 1000 students were surveyed, that more than half said they'd been victims or Racism, and Prof Iyiola Solanke, the dean for equality, diversity and inclusion at the University of Leeds, told a seminar on the report hosted by the Higher Education Policy Institute that she was surprised that many of the instances of racism hadn't changed from when she was an undergraduate, when other students expected her to be a drug dealer or to like hip-hop.

Racism in the UK is not as apparent as that in Germany where an African-styled Bantu hair is the most befitting representation of the novel coronavirus—a 'Black' girl in her full African regalia, they think, sends the right preventive message from the coronavirus. Reacting to this may prove juvenile in broad sense as it's not a self-contained act in itself but one of the many reasons the typical may grow up with, and may have to choose one day whether the 'Black' is fitful of their friendship; it won't sound racist if racism is how these societies train a privileged sect, when it says the privileged are so because of their skin pigmentation.

It feels obscene that we tackle racism like it's what will *just* disappear when a small African boy in a corner of Oxfordshire *still* watches the recurring motif of Barbie, a sweet white girl (with Black minor character), the adventures of Tarzan, though this African boy, let's assume, have never come in contact with the fair-colored, already has been institutionalized into the White-Validating culture.

Fanon has this to say:

"We are entitled, however, to ask how total identification with the white man can still be the case in the twentieth century? Very often the black man who becomes abnormal has never come into contact with Whites. Has some former experience been repressed in his unconscious? Has the young black child seen his father beaten or lynched by the white man? Has there been a real traumatism? To all these questions our answer is *no*. So where do we go from here?" [6]

Identification with Whitness began quite early. Catholicism, in Nigeria for example, emphasizes on the evils of Black in relation to Satan and the end of the world; Books go along to topicalize on Blackness in relation to the Africa continent, so many Souls of the Black Fold running wild; Whiteness represents God; Religion emphasizes this— all religions began on the altar of color segregation. How does the Negro—in its very word! —distinguish himself from Satanism and Ire so vivid in the films, and news and experiences that conditions him? The path to salvation, then, becomes identification with God, with Whiteness, and to be denied this access to God is to deny his moral inclinations, his 'Ought,' his individualism, and by simply 'striking the first and only blow' he sees it as a 'legitimate defense.'[7] (G. Legman.)

Identification with Whiteness comes off as basic; inclination to Western-styled houses, the divorce of the native language because it sounds like rattling, the investment into the English language, etc! This African boy who lived in identification with Whiteness, the 'good' of every movie he watched, would inevitably come to the conclusion that the very Blackness he'd detested was him; he was the Blackness. Two things are subsequently set before him, which arises during the years spent in limbo between identity: is his self-will strong enough to resist convention, to resist turning to crime? Would it matter anyway if he turns to crime if, in the long run, he would be a criminal, whether or not he has criminal records? And had he done wrong by seeking to elevate his undeserving by going to College—though his political appointments is limited—yet he does something tangible in the tech industry, or in the Sciences, or in the Sports, or even with 'White' children—yet he suffers, this College boy who is a Scientist or an excellent sportsman—he suffers being one day called, "a black Scientist," or a 'Black' headnews running wild, "Blacks are winning everywhere." He does not have a choice than accept the life before him, his role in history, his responsibility to 'Blackness' first before anything.

He has to find solace and companionship in the

Color bar. Only there would he find other 'Black' College boys who'd been doing, achieving for the 'Black' community; there he becomes part of the Resistance, he becomes another 'Black kid' from Tennessee or South Side Chicago; there, this 'Black folk' can be 'Black, and artistic, and beautiful.'

He resists the Resistance only to his own mishap. He may be fair-skinned, still he's part African and will suffer racism. He may want to dissociate himself from 'Blacker' Africans from Togo or Madagascar, he may, ostensibly, want to self-isolate from 'otherness,' thus, he becomes a recluse—

Before I proceed, it's imperative I quote Fanon saying:

"A normal black child, having grown up with a normal family, will become abnormal at the slightest contact with the white world."

And for why this College boy may turn sociopathic, Sigmund Freud says:

"In almost every case, we could see that the symptoms were, so to speak, like residues of emotional experiences, to which for this reason we gave the name of psychic traumas… In contrast, however, to what was expected, it was not always a single event that was the cause of the symptom; most often, on the contrary, it arose out of multiple traumas, frequently analogous and repeated."[8]

This 'Negro' becomes violent to navigate his any human innate tendency to crime, partly because he feels isolated and he has no moral inclination towards the legal institution. Little, unfortunately, does 'Black communities' do to curb this isolation. Thus, a British is British until he reacts to racial injustices and becomes a 'Black-' or 'Brown-British,' when self-doubts set in.

Whether these 'Black' communities, serving as freedom from the outside world, are social palatableness is argumentative; whether they should exist remains a question a playwright of some 'other' species will answer one day.

Except that, these communities say what the common African should not be— "not be less," they say— but what this 'Black' boy should be without his Blackness, these communities have not said. Romanticizing the Color Bar becomes ideal: *Black is beautiful. Black doesn't crack. Black, Art.* And I dare ask what parameters qualify Blackness as blackness— what rule(s)? Who sets those rules? Shouldn't these rules be the very enemy? Shouldn't the cancellation of labeling be an *ideal* thing? And if the White-system reportedly colonized Africa, once (is), should that be a moral judgment on the African living permanently, or not, in the Diaspora (ought)? What efforts do deductive reasoning as this play on Psychology and socio-cultural representation? How would the esoteric Congolese surcease prohibitive racism on their own— with or without an Independence treaty, or a Black Landmark… act—?

The Congolese or Chinese-Congolese must note in this case that the contrastive, inimical 'Black literary genealogy' must be done away with, as it reminds him of a supposedly 'Black legacy,' a 'Black history,' the substance of his discontentment.

Louis Gates emphasizes this when he said:

"Literary works configure into a tradition not because of some mystical collective unconscious determined by the biology of race or gender, but because writers read other writers and ground their representations of experience in models of language provided largely by other writers to whom they feel akin." [9]

In conclusion, nothing is beautiful in Blackness. There should be no Romanticization! Blackness is just black, pale, and it doesn't crack because blackness is not the body of a human. People with African descent will not crack because of biological and climate coincidences. Non-Africans, too, will not crack as easily. Blackness should be destroyed not sexed!

CHAPTER 6

WHEN WILL THE BRITISH ACCEPT THEY ARE THIEVES?

Prior to the colonial rule in Africa and during that period, countless of the continent's cultural artefacts and other valuables were nefariously plundered. It is interesting to learn that it is often remarked that the British Museum was the first of a new kind of museum, which means that it is national and does not belong to church or king. However, centuries later(1900 – 1925), it became apparent to even ignoramuses and simpletons that the British Museum, despite its seemingly benign façade, it had inexorably aggressive intention to rob African countries of their artefacts and valuables to furnish the British Museum and enrich the British culture.

This British museum is one of the biggest no-human thieves in world's history. There was something Geoffrey Robertson QC said, which I find interesting, and hope you will. He said: "The trustees of the British Museum have become the world's largest receivers of stolen property, and the great majority of their loot is not even on public display."

He criticized the museum for allowing an unofficial "stolen goods tour". This tour stops at the Elgin marbles, Hoa Hakananai'a, the Benin bronzes and other stolen goods.

At the expiration of the 19th century, "The British Museum's collections had increased to the extent that its building was no longer large enough." The word is "collections", but the most accurate phrase is "stolen goods." They were stolen and people who steal are thrives, aren't they? The British Museum is a house filled to the brim with stolen goods and thieves. Emil Torday, to begin with, was a thief, though he had a curious respect for Africans and while in Congo "discovered" a kingdom he though was partake with European dynasties. He even cultivated a good relationship with nyimi(king) KotaPe/Kwete of the Kuba Kingdom, but he was a thief. He was a their who journeyed to Africa in the early 1900s to steal, under the auspices of the British Museum. He visited the Congo thrice(the last in 1908) and looted three times. His meeting with Thomas Athol Joyce, worked for the British Museum, amplified his interests in anthropology and, yes, theft. The British Museum sent him back to the Belgian Congo, where, in the Kwango River Basin, he amassed "a collection of 3000 objects from the Kuba Kingdom for the museum. Other outstanding pieces of the collection are three royal Ndop figures he collected. "(Emil Torday, at the British Museum/Wikipedia). But today, unfortunately, the criminal's THEFT was recognized in 1910 as he was awarded the Imperial Gold Medal for Science and Art by the emperor of Austria. In 2020, participants of the Budapest – Bamako charity rally named a school after him in Sierra Leone. Why?

The most unforgivable crime by the British Museum was the looting of the Kingdom of Benin in my country Nigeria. 900 objects in this kingdom were brazenly looted by the British military whose appetite for loot is unrivalled in the annals of colonial pillaging. Some of these exhibits stolen from Benin City by a British military force in 1897 were the breathtaking Benin bronzes. It's sad that all these were stolen, the Royal Palace razed to the ground, and yet the British

Museum do not want to accept the fact that they are criminals, thieves, bandits, who are yet to answer for their criminality against my people. It's sad that the Benin shrines were stolen by the British forces and innumerable objects of ceremonial or ritual value shipped to the UK. It's pathetic that the artefacts were not only given to this criminally-minded museum but were also sold at auction or kept by soldiers for their mantelpieces. It's pathetic that two ivory leopards of great value, stolen from the innocent Africans, were given to the criminally and shamelessly beatified Queen Victoria. These atrocities happened to the people of Benin because the thieves considered the folks from "The Heart of Darkness" inferior, subhuman and unintelligent. But why can't they, the people stealing for the museum, accept the glaringly obvious fact that they are thieves? It is important that they accept their status as thieves, imperial pillagers, unrestrained criminals, because their criminal identity has not changed. After their theft in 1897, many of the stolen goods were purchased by museums in Germany, Austria, and the United States. Unsurprisingly, some of them even ended up in private collections. Many historians believe that the renowned Spanish painter Pablo Picasso, another beatified criminal, owned one.

Oh, Egypt. Egypt, like Nigeria and Congo, was also a victim of the British Museum's criminal inclination and adventures. That 1. 12m (3ft 6in) high Rosetta Stone in the British Museum is originally from Egypt. On 22 November 2018, Ashley Line, writing for BBC Africa, Nairobi, asserted that it is "unclear how the stone was discovered in July 1799, but there's a general belief that it was found by soldiers fighting with the French military leader Napoleon Bonaparte as they were building an extension to a fort near the twin of Rashid – also known as Rosetta – in Nile Delta. "

He went further to reveal or remind us that after Napoleon was defeated, the British seized the stone under the terms of the Treaty of Alexandria in 1801.

He arrived in Portsmouth, England, in February 1802 and George III offered it to the British Museum a few months later.

There was a British explorer called Richard Lander who removed the first artefact from Nigeria during British's process of colonisation. This valuable was an intricately carved Yoruba stool that is ironically now named after Lander and held in this thief that is the British Museum. There are also stolen artefacts from other parts of the world, including the Parthenon Sculptures, a collection of marble architectural decoration from the Acropolis in Athens, Greece.

These Parthenon Sculptures are a collection of different types of marble architectural decorations from the temple of Athena. It was made between 442 BC and 432 BC. The Ottoman Empire, which was the governing authority in Athens for 350 years, made Lord Elgins the British Ambassador. He ordered the removal of figures. He removed about half of the Parthenon. Even the sculptural and architectural elements from several buildings on the Acropolis. All of this Pink thief's collections of antiquities were shipped to Britain, and Act of Parliament gave its permission to have them entered into the British Museum.

Magdala Ethiopian Treasures were mercilessly

looted. This was during a battle, and this battle was called the battle of the Magdala in 1868, and the criminal Britain triumphed. This victory enabled them to steal thousands of valuable items treasured by the Ethiopian Empire. They stole innumerable valuables and had to use "15 elephants and thousands of miles to transport the goods to a nearby town for auction." Richard. Holmes, another criminal element, was one of the attendees. Under the auspices of the British Museum he "purchased hundreds of manuscripts, an intricately woven royal wedding gown, and the much-coveted Crown of Abud – a good crown that once sat stop The head of the leader of the Ethiopian Church."

The valuables ended up in the Victoria and Albert Museum, but Richard Holmes of the British Museum enabled this nefarious looting, duly representing his criminally minded country.

The British Museum also stole from the Gold Coast (now Ghana). The cultural property, which they pilfered, was a valuable drum. Ernest Domfeh, a Ghanaian drummer and dancer, told VICE World News that the drum from this museum is an Akan drum and it is from Ashanti, Ghana. "It is from my people," he stated. "I think it is a drum that could be taken during the time of the king of Ashanti, Prempeh I.. . Back then the British were overlords of the Ashanti s because they were our colonial masters. They thought the Ashanti were powerful, so they needed to take hold of what is their source of power, so they could become powerless for them to rule them entirely." Apparently Britain's appetite suffers the worst battering if denied loot from Africa or other parts of the world.

The British thefts in India are some of the most interesting ones. The hallowed Ring of Tipu Sultan was stolen by the Pinks. There was a war in the late seventeen century, which this ruler of Mysore (also called the Tiger of Mysore) lost in 1799. The British colonialists, better called criminal pillagers, stole this treasured sword and his ring from his body. Fortunately, the sword was returned to India in 2004, but the ring was auctioned by the British for "£145,000. The 41.2g ring was sold to an undisclosed bidder for almost 10 times its estimated price at the auction in central London, according to Christie's website. The jewelled ring is inscribed with the name of Hindu God Ram in raised Devanagari inscribed on it." Talk about a shameless pillager!

Amaravati marbles are still on display at this criminally-minded British Museum; a pillager relic that ought to be pulled down and reduced to ashes. The theft? We are talking about a collection of seventy pieces depicting India's cherished and famous Amaravati sculptures brazenly inaugurated at the British Museum. Bhuspinder Singh, an Indian writer, wrote in Indian Times, that it was excavated by the British almost 140 years ago, and the sculptures were transported to the Great Britain from Madras in 1859. These sculptures remained in the basement of the museum for over thirty years.

The Great Britain is a civilised nation, and in civilised nations, the law does not allow a thief to keep let alone flaunt and exhibit his or her looted goods, even if such goods were stolen one hundred years ago. However, the British Museum, as I have said earlier and will certainly continue to say, is a thief, a shameless thief that is shamelessly celebrated by shameless people. The criminal cast of the British Museum certainly says a lot about the entire country. Perhaps civilization is nothing but beatified criminality. Why do the British claim to be civilised, just and lawful, and yet they do not want to return all the cultural properties stolen from Africa, India and other places round the globe?

Not long ago, in 2017, President Macron of France remarked that "African cultural heritage can no longer remain a prisoner of European museums." The honest leader was keen on sending back to Nigeria some of the Benin Bronzes, bought by the French after they were seized in a barbaric punishment raid by the pillagers in the British army in 1897. As we breathe today, the France of President Emmanuel Macron, is the only European nation with looted artifacts that is inclined to listen to these urgent calls for repatriation. He once promised that the Quai Branly Museum in Paris will return twenty stolen valuables to Benin (the African country, and not the Benin Kingdom in Nigeria). I like that Mr. Macron promised this and also promised to alter the French law so that his country will return stolen objects whenever the robbed nation asks for them. But the British Museum, this relic of a beatified pillager we are discussing in this chapter, has unabashedly disclosed that it has zero interest in returning all the stolen artifacts. Some beautiful people like to say criminals change, but from what we know, they definitely have anyone but Britain in mind.

Nigeria my country has been asking the United Kingdom to return our Benin bronzes for decades, most times we are greeted with cold silence. Perhaps the brazen thieves thought we are foolish, or they were paralyzed with guilt and trepidation? Whatever it was that made them treat us the way they treated us, I am glad that we were not discouraged or intimidated; we continued to write, and in 2018, the British Museum agreed to send some bronzes to my country for the Royal Museum we planned to open last year(2021). Do you know on what grounds? The idiots remarked that it is only "loaning" the sculptures to Nigeria. This madness meant that they expected the country they ravaged and raped to return the goods they pillaged to them? How can one person be idiotic, heartless and shameless at the same time? In a fabulous essay (Will the British Museum Ever Return Stolen Artifacts) written by Becky Little and published in History on December 21, 2018, I learnt that that period the British Museum announced that it would loan Nigeria its own artifacts, "a protest theatre group called "BP Or Not BP?" organized a "Stolen Goods Tour" at the British Museum. The tour highlighted artifacts like the Gwaegal shield, which the British stole from Aboriginal Australians in the late 18th century. Similarly, to the Benin bronzes, the British Museum refused to repatriate the Gwaegal shield to Australia for a 2016 museum exhibit. Instead, the British Museum loaned the shield and reclaimed it afterward."

This word, "loaned", is very stupid, ridiculous, and quite undeniably convincing as to the brazen unrepentance of the Great Pillager called Britain. I detest it in that speech and I detest that the speech was ever made public. The British Museum Director Hartwig Fischer once told the *The New York Times* that "the collections have to be preserved as whole." What utter rubbish from a wazzock! You don't preserve stolen goods; you return stolen goods to the owner or owners, you moppet! Again, a thief, when caught, should return his or stolen goods – or be forced to return them. If the former is hard for the pillager, the victims must make sure the full wrath of the latter does not escape the pillager! The British Museum is a thief we have caught and demand that it returns people's stolen goods. Can't the British Prime Minister follow the footsteps of France's president, Emmanuel Macron who has already promised to return the artifacts France stole from Nigeria and some other African countries? If he does not do that, it is our collective duty to force the hand of the pillager!

CHAPTER SEVEN

IF YOU SPEAK UP AGAINST THE EMPIRE, YOU WILL BE CANCELED

In September 2007, there was a conference commemorating the 40th anniversary of the demise of the illustrious poet, Christopher Okigbo. It was an event for which we cannot pencil down a precise date, but which is believed to have occurred sometime in September 1967 amid the horrors of the Nigerian civil war.

The relevant facts of the conference to this essay are reconstructed, retrospectively, by this author from panoply of sources, a press release and a series of YouTube video clips. From this piecemeal assemblage of sources, one detects that the conference brought together the most venerable, living minds in the Nigerian literary and humanities intelligentsia.

In Nigerian literatures post-colonial era, the famous Mbari quartet Achebe, Clark, Okigbo, Soyinka constitutes some of the most revered names. Two of the three living members of that quartet, at the time, were present and accounted for at the conference to honor their comrade. The absence of JP Clark from the conference proceedings remains a mystery to this writer.

The organizers, in their wisdom, scheduled both Soyinka and Achebe to deliver their keynote addresses on the third day of the conference. Soyinka's presentation was timed for the morning hours and Achebe's for the afternoon. In making his presentation, the Nobel laureate rejected the impulse to construct a discourse in the abstract on Okigbo's literary legacy. He preferred to acquaint the audience with some of the salient details of his intimacy with

Okigbo. Set against the backdrop of the publication of his memoir, You Must Set Forth at Dawn a year earlier, it seemed a most appropriate choice. Then came the Q&A session, during which the signal event that helped anchor my conversation occurred.

Accompanying one of the questions posed to Soyinka was a prefatory remark that elicited a memorable response from the man regarded fondly among the Nigerian literati as Kongi. It ran thus: I know you are very patriotic Nigerian It remains exasperatingly difficult, watching the YouTube clip, to make out the full outlines of the question asked. [The organizers, perhaps considering the relatively small size of the room, had dropped the ball on a crucial conference technicality: microphones had not been made available to members of the audience to ask their questions or make their contributions as they were.] However, it is detectable from fragments of the conversation that the question revolved around the activities of the Movement for the Actualization of the Sovereign State of Biafra (MASSOB) and other regional, centrifugal forces tearing at the Nigerian state at the time.

It was not in answering that question but the one that followed that Soyinka found an appropriate context to rebuff the notion that he was a patriot.

Gesturing to the gentleman who had posed the earlier question, he said, in part: "…You call me patriotic. I am not really a patriot, you know. I don't have that sense of, eh, of patriotism. I believe in human beings. I believe that the human community transcends, as one would recognize it, that issue of identity That it transcends national boundaries, especially boundaries which are so artificial, which were imposed on peoples, not in their own interest, but as productive entities to service the industrial requirements of imperialist nations

It was the first but not, so far, the last time that I would hear Soyinka put up a protest against those who sang the praises of his alleged Nigerian patriotism. And this insistence on pushing back against the attribution of this civic virtue to him weaves into his broader critique of the dangers of the romanticism and fervor that attends the nation-state formation, and the crimes that those nationalistic passions have led to. Speaking to an Italian magazine in 2016, he took this critique up a notch, arguing that nations constitute the worst single crime against humanity of which humanity is guilty, fortunately only against itself.

So, in Soyinka's reckoning, the human community supersedes the nation. What inspires his political action is a certain allegiance to the human condition that takes expression within his immediate political constituency Nigeria and way beyond it. Allegiance to the human condition entails an insistence on humanity first, before any of the identity structures that convey the particulars of human existence: race, ethnicity, nationality, religion. In its most virtuous manifestation, it is leavened by love, indiscriminate love. This expression of love extends beyond the boundaries defined by these identity-based allegiances. It consciously embraces the other and insists on the mutual reinforcement of love for the other by love for one's own.

Soyinka's defined allegiance to the human condition as transcending communities of defined identities reads, in retrospect, as an indictment of the nativism and nationalism sweeping large swathes of the world today in varying degrees of intensity across the North Atlantic democracies, with the exception of Canada (for now), but also in places as far flung as India under Modi, and in the coming to power of right-wing nationalists in the Slavic regions of East and Central Europe, Poland and Hungary most especially. In the western democracies straddled by the Atlantic as well as among their Slavic friends, the linchpin issue is immigration and nativism takes the form of political movements organized around the anti-immigrant sentiment.

There is, however, another more constructive political development that has attended this wave of nationalism the resurgence of devolution as one of the most potent political forces acting within and beyond nation-state boundaries. From Catalonia in Spain to Kurdish Iraq, two longstanding secessionist movements have forced the issue of independence referendums in 2017 alone, despite strong, even brutal, opposition from the national governments whose rule they seek to be free from. Calls for what might have been 2017s third major referendum by the resurgent secessionist movement seeking independence for the state of Biafra from Nigeria have been ignored and suppressed. British politics has been complicated in recent years by the occurrence, first, of the Scottish Independence referendum in 2014, which failed to break up the United Kingdom, and by the choice made by a plurality of British voters to exit the European Union last year. The nationalist spirit, or more precisely, the ethnic spirit, is having its field day and the eruptions are ongoing.

How does the liberal-minded social commentator, of the caste of Soyinka, respond to the political consequences of these trends? Would any given responses (not) be prone to contradictions?

The answers to these may lie in the way in which the commentator triangulates between the two value systems that are placed on a collision course by these developments. In considering an agitation for secession, one may choose to lend one's voice to the imperative of self-determination for people who consider themselves trapped in an oppressive or dysfunctional political unit. Or one might worry that the legitimacy of the right to self-determination notwithstanding, the world is being dangerously led to ruin by rabid nationalism, underpinned by nativism and xenophobia, and that under those conditions, it is better to do what is democratically possible to avert the break-up of large, multicultural, multiethnic political units. In post-referendum Catalonia in October, 'pro-unity' rallies organized by locals who preferred to continue to be citizens of Spain one wonders where they were when the actual votes were cast had among their leading voices, the Peruvian novelist and Nobel laureate, Mario Vargas Llosa. His rationale? The necessity of pushing back against the dangers of rising nationalism.

Let us look at Nigeria and the resurgent Biafran struggle, which is our test case, and to Wole Soyinka's interactions with that struggle and the irruptions it has spawned. Sometime in 1967, as the storms of the Nigerian civil war gathered hostilities had begun under conditions of what was euphemistically termed police action on the Federal side, with a loose blockade having been imposed on the secessionist enclave Biafra by the Nigerian military, Soyinka undertook an expedition, beginning from Lagos, into the enclave on a mission to persuade Col. Emeka Odumegwu Ojukwu, erstwhile military governor of the defunct Eastern region and leader of the aspiring independent republic of Biafra, to revoke the declaration of secession made earlier that year, cease hostilities and facilitate a return to the conference table with the Nigerian state.

This exercise in daredevilry ultimately ended up in his arrest and prolonged detention for 27 months, 20 in solitary confinement, for a duration approximating the rest of the civil war. And it is one of the signal events in what is Soyinka's complicated relationship complicated by virtue of disparities in perception with Ndigbo. Predictably, the horrors of the Nigerian civil war expose the ethnic fault lines of the Nigerian nation-state to a degree unmatched by any other event in the country's history. The fraught relationship between the ethnic nationalities in the southern

Nigeria, the Igbo and the Yoruba most especially, and the dominant Hausa-Fulani nationalities in the north are well known. Between the Igbo and the Yoruba, however, the details of that war are discussed; they are even taught to future generations, for they are a source of heightened emotionalism that revives recriminations between two nationalities whose destinies, some would argue, are inextricably linked.

2017 marked the 50th anniversary of the commencement of that war and as such presented a symbolic and sentimental climate into which the energies unleashed by the surviving aspiration of secession among the Igbo, under the romantic political unit, Biafra, could reach its peak since the war ended. Resurgent agitations for the realization of the Biafran state have imposed a responsibility on the most qualified discussants of the civil war to steer the national conversation. A couple of developments in the lead up to 2017 have colored the ways in which Soyinka's rightful contributions to this discourse as a Yoruba man have been perceived among the Igbo.

There is the suggestion that his absence at his legendary colleague, Chinua Achebe's burial in 2013, was an indication of ill will towards Achebe. Purveyors of that canard got a blistering rejoinder. Then there was Soyinkagate, the invention and dissemination of a derogatory quote about Ndigbo attributed to Soyinka as having been uttered at a lecture at the Hutchins Institute, Harvard University, in 2015. He was even more acerbic with this cast of mischief-makers.

We may classify Soyinka's mission to Biafra as one of his active interventions' in humanity's affairs, as opposed to the literary corpus of his Interventions Series (IVII), the collections of essays which he has produced since the mid-2000s to address festering, vexing issues that continue to exercise his recreative tempers in the Nigerian space and beyond. The Biafran episode stands out, among the active interventions that Soyinka has made in various political conflicts around the world as interlocutor between dueling groups, as the one closest to home. South Africa in the early 1990s, notably to facilitate reconciliation and eventual synergy between Nelson Mandela's Africa National Congress and Mangosuthu Buthelezis Inkatha Freedom Party, but also and more peripherally, Israel-Palestine and even Cuba are only some examples. The common denominator running through these interventions is the allegiance to the human condition.

And there is a central tenet that serves as the wellspring of inspiration for these interventions transcendental JUSTICE. This is a virtue he has described as the first condition of humanity. Whatever perceptions are held, and by whomever, about the nature of Soyinka's feelings towards the Igbo, the following are indisputable.

He has not wavered in calling the 1966 pogroms against Ndigbo in Northern Nigeria a genocide. In defiance of the Nigerian officialdom, he dismisses what he called (in an article in July for American newsmagazine, Newsweek) its wishfully terminal mantra invoked in response to heightened calls for a referendum on the potential independence of the Biafran state, that Nigeria's unity is non-negotiable.

As one of the leading luminaries called upon to help navigate a national reckoning with the horrors of the Asaba Massacre of October 1967 at the 50th anniversary remembrance colloquium, Soyinka memorably reprised the substance of his disagreement with his distinguished friends in the Rainbow Nation Nelson Mandela and Archbishop Desmond Tutu over South Africa's Truth and Reconciliation Commission. [In The Burden of Memory, the Muse of Forgiveness, Soyinka famously criticized the methods of the TRC for letting Apartheid South Africa's malefactors off without imposing any burden of reparation. Tutus defence of the TRCs methods is presented in his purposefully named No Future Without Forgiveness.]

"In Asaba", Soyinka, invoking his disagreement with Tutu, queried, I can say to Bishop Tutu, I have found forgiveness But I can also ask: where is restitution? The profundity of the tribute to the big-heartedness of the Igbo victims of that tragedy and the poignant assertion of what is owed them is heartwarming.

Still his preferred outcome for the resolution of the Nigerian national question is for the continued existence of the union. In the already referenced Newsweek article, Soyinka asks, regarding the Biafra aspiration: Should Biafra stay in, or opt out of Nigeria? That is the latent question. Even after years of turbulent co-tenancy, it seems unreal to conceive of a Nigeria without Biafra. My preference for in goes beyond objective assessment of economic, cultural and social advantages for Biafra and the rest of us.

He then adds, to firm up the argument: Among many analogies, I have heard and read Nigeria described as a ticking time-bomb. Ironically, I see in this very fear a strong argument for remaining intact. An explosion in closed space is deadlier than in a wider arena which stands a chance of diffusing the impact and enabling survival. My preference for remaining one is thus reinforced by that very doomsday prediction, not by any presumptive law of human association.

In lending his creative prowess to the realization of his preference for the continued existence of multi-ethnic, multi-textual Nigeria, he occupies a common front as does his fellow Nobel laureate, Vargas Llosa. In his insistence on the legitimacy and righteousness of the right to self-determination for the Igbos and any political actions that may arise therefrom, Soyinka parts with Llosa.

For an individual, one individual, to be said to have a special relationship, good or bad, with an entire ethnic nationality, a large, dynamic, peripatetic one such as the Igbo nonetheless, based on antecedent histories, is an uncommon story, often the preserve of society's biggest influencers. Commoner expressions of ethnic identity-subverting allegiance to the human condition has to consist in the quality of personal relationships. Unable to effectively assess the millions of interactions between ordinary individuals across ethnic boundaries, society relies on the quality of relationships between the elites in the various ethnicities to reflect the overall sense of the health of group interaction this is besides reliance on data on gruesome conflicts or major touchstones of inter-group tension.

This, perhaps, accounts for the fixation among Nigerians, especially Igbo and Yoruba, on the nature of the relationship between Soyinka and Achebe, and indeed among the members, living and dead, of the Mbari quartet. Curiosity about the nature of the Soyinka-Achebe relationship coexists with the difficult-to-control impulse to compare them the quality of their work, their accomplishments. It is an exercise that often exposes deep-seated ethnic loyalties, but also, and not so irregularly, preferences that buck the trend of ethnic loyalty.

Within this writers' circle of friends are a number of literary enthusiasts of Yoruba extraction, two especially come to mind, who complain of the inaccessibility of Soyinka's literary style vis-à-vis Achebe, ultimately settling on a preference for the latter. As an Igbo man, I often feel the impulse to rationalize my preference for the former, for I am personally acquainted with him. The answer lies in timing of their respective exertions of influence on my literary and intellectual palette. I read Achebe mostly as a child and, somewhat later, as a teenager.

The consequence was that I approached his works with the limitations of the childhood intelligence, unable to grasp their full import. On the other hand, Soyinka's essayistic interventions in the affairs of Nigeria and climes beyond have been a recurring decimal in my intellectual formation in the crucial late teen-early adulthood years.

In conclusion, I want to reiterate that the general atmosphere in Haiti is symptomatic of other issues: the unwillingness to put paid to gainless political turmoil, economic meanderings and cultural immolation is damaging the prospects of the nation's prosperity. We are familiar with the extraordinary journey of Haiti from revolution to independence in the early nineteenth century, and we are conversant with the movement that propelled her to the apotheosis of anti-imperial paragon among other countries reeling from the rapaciousness and bestiality of European empires. We iterate, also, our cognizance of the season of turmoil, which some people would argue has been rather perennial than periodical; that led to the truncation of several governments and the notoriety of Haiti as one of the foremost among a handful of countries with the highest number of coups d'état globally.

The question now is what exactly Haiti needs: more vexatious undulations or tangible progressive actions? The answer lies in whom we ask or where we look. There is a school of thought proselytizing the exaction of reparation from European nations to Haiti.

The argument here was noted earlier and it anchors on paying reparations to Haiti for the many years of slavery, unpaid labor, dehumanization on slave plantations, encomienda systems, and so on by European nations. The other school of thought, which is pragmatic, concerns the centralization of the human condition, the ultimate universal, as a propelling force in policy-making and the attainment of political consensus. An undertaking of sweeping political arbitraments, as a prelude to rapid socio-economic developments, cultural revitalization, and tangible improvement in the human condition, is urgently required. If pursued meticulously, such undertaking can alter the mode of Haitian transition from etiolation to rejuvenation. The combination of improved infrastructure, government services in marginalized areas inside and outside of Port-au-Prince, jobs and education for at-risk youth, and robust law enforcement can reduce the propensity toward violence in these areas, if they are sustained for sufficient time and linked to longer-term development.

CHAPTER EIGHT

WE OWE THE BRITISH EMPIRE SOME GRATITUDE

The history of the world has been the one of empires. Think the Mongols, think the Ottomans, and, most especially, the British. The British exploitation in guise of colonialism is sadly interesting. The British have colonies in Africa, Australia, and the Americas. These colonies played – and continue to play—vital roles in the economy of the British people. Their empire, unfortunately, could not restrain them from shipping their people, artefacts, capital, ideas, and capital to their own nation. The most forlorn part of this ugly experience was not the frequent movements of the colonies' valuables, but also the opportunity it granted the Pinks to force their Western ideology on us Africans –now our people speak their language, write in their language, think in their language, worship their Christian God, use their Greenwich Mean Time(which they introduced to our ancestors in 1847). How can I possibly forget and forgive the fact that the Pinks, or the colonial masters, jettisoned the unique and beautiful ways of life of the indigenous people of Africa, Asia, and Oceania, which they obviously and unabashedly thought backward and barbaric, and imposed theirs not to "help" them but for their own selfish interest.

Prior to explicating why, I think we owe the British Empire some gratitude, let us examine some of the colonial evils done to the British Empire by the British people for the British.

1. The Kenyan Camps

When the people of Kenya aired their desire to have their country back in the 1950s, the British rounded up 1.5 million natives and locked them up in concentration camps. The slogan was "labor and freedom", and the inmates worked as slaves filling in mass graves. Many of these inmates(the official count is approximately 2, 000) were killed by stuffing their mouths with mud, burning them alive or stamping on their throats. What was their "crime", you ask? They were aiding the "rebels". And anybody who stood in the way of the British imperialism and exploitation of Kenya must be brought down. But, fortunately I or Kenya, unfortunately for Britain, the innocent African country gained freedom in 1963.

This unforgettable atrocity, among many other atrocities carried out by the British colonialists in Africa, would not have happened if the British had let Kenya alone. But their desire to impoverish Africa and ship our valuables to their country was intense. In 2019, Max Bearak wrote a brilliant article for the Washington Post about the Pokomo people of Kenya and the Tana River valley, which was one worshiped by a god represented on Earth by an "awe-inspiring" drum. It stood "taller than any man", this drum, and rubbing the cowhide stretched across its gigantic body made from tree trunk, "made a sound that could be heard through the villages clustered around the Pokomo's king's compound."

Consider this relatively lengthy but pertinent extract from this article of Max Bearak's:

"Our legend has it that it sounds like a lion's roar," said His Majesty Makorani-a-Mungase VII, the current Pokomo

king and the descendant of a dynasty he claims goes back more than a dozen generations. "It forced everyone to listen. It was alive."

That drum, the ngadji, the source of power and pride for the Pokomo, has been relegated to a storage room in the British Museum in London for 111 years.

The theft of the ngadji by British colonial officers is a story well-known among the eldest Pokomo. The British Museum, too, acknowledges the ngadji was "confiscated" before being donated to its collections in 1908. The museum also acknowledges a request by the Pokomo community for its return.

So why is the ngadji in a closet in London, rather than in Mchelelo, Makorani's sacred grove along a bend in the Tana River?

The answer, Max went further to explain, lies in the heated debate in Western museums:

[W] here halls are filled with the riches of plundered lands, over whether institutions that benefited from colonialism have any right to keep such collections long into the postcolonial era.

To the British Museum and others, even ill-gotten artifacts are now their property. The argument is a legal and utilitarian one: This is where the items are safest and most people will see them.

"The British Museum takes its commitment to being

a world museum seriously," said Nicola Elvin, a British Museum spokeswoman, in an emailed statement. She added that objects the museum holds are viewed by millions of visitors. "The Trustees of the British Museum have always been clear that they will consider (subject to the usual considerations of condition and fitness to travel) any loan request for any part of the collection."

In this very article, a supposedly saddened Kenya said, "If you combined Britain's parliamentary mace and the Queen's crown jewels, you would still not equal the amount of cultural significance the ngadji had for us. Its loss has stripped us of our sense of who we are."

In this article, I discovered, with a shudder, that the king's brother(a London-based man) was granted access to the drum by the British Museum and is now the first person in his community to touch it in over a century. Touched or untouched, the drum is still in the UK and "roughly 200, 000 Pokomo have now converted to Islam and Christianity, including the royal family."

2. The Partitioning of India and Other Atrocities

Have you ever heard of the Pink man, Cyril Radcliffe? This man was a servant of the British Empire in 1947. When, over lunch, he was asked to draw the border between India and the newly created Pakistan, he foolishly, wickedly, obeyed. This border, which Cyril Radcliffe made to split the subcontinent along religious lines, was a ludicrous. Neither Hindus in modern Pakistan nor Muslims in modern India wanted to be in the wrong side; they – about 30 million people—struggled frantically, desperately, to flee, but it ended in religious violence and gruesome killings. Innumerable houses were ransacked and razed down with the villages.

The artefacts that the British confiscated, looted or took as presents in India include the Buddha's shrine from the Amaravati monument, the 105.6- karat "koh – i –noor" diamond, which adorned Queen Victoria's brooch, the Queen Mother's crown, and a wooden tiger. Today these cultural valuables are displaced in the British Museum (and in other museums like the Pitt Museum and the Victoria and Albert Museum.

3. Boer Concentration Camps

The Great Britain invaded the Boer republic's and camps were established as part of their military campaign against two small Afrikaner republics, which were the ZAR(Transvaal) and the Orange Free State. Actually, it was the British Army that created the concentration camps. It was as part of a against Boer takeover of their independent republic. Between June 1901 and May 1902, virtually 28, 000 people died – 22, 000 of them were children. In the end, it is recorded that about 20, 000 "Black people" died in other camps. All these innocent people lost their lives because the British wanted to get "Black people" odd the land; they also wanted them as labourers on gold mines. This is to show that the Pink man's urge to steal from the country their own called "The Heart of Darkness" is ancient. This is unforgivable ass it sapped the people and helped the British economically.

They steal lives, steal gold mines, they steal human beings, steal artifacts and steal other goods of immense cultural and economic values. Many of which end up in European museums, especially in the British Museum.

Apparently, museums have a major impact to local and national economies. With continued support from Local Authorities, DCMS and other public and private funders, museums can play an ever more important role in our economy and communities. This report examines the economic impact of museums to England, and it finds that the museums sector:

1. generates £2.64 billion in income
2. contributes £1.45 billion in economic output to the national economy
3. employs a minimum of 38,165 people is made up of approximately 2,635 organizations running 2,720 sites across England
4. is estimated to generate £3 of income (including earned income, income from investments, grants from charities and foundations, and donations, etc.) for each £1 of public sector grant.

Number One says that museums generate £ 2. 64 billion in income. The main museum here, the most important museum here, is the British Museum. This amount, 2. 64, is undeniably massive. It is necessary to remind us that several African countries, where many of these income-generating treasures were stolen, do not even make half of this in two or more years. This is a naked case of economic rape and those who defend it deserve to burn in everlasting furnace! The British Museum raped Nigeria, raped Kenya, raped India, raped Sierra Leone and several other colonies, and yet they the Pink folks do not want to show their gratitude for our unintentional financial assistance and admit that they are rapists and pillagers who are living better lives because of Africa and some parts of Asia. Sometimes I wonder where the Great Britain would have been if her brazenly criminal ancestors had not done the wicked things, they did to the countries they colonised.

Number Two says that museums (especially the British Museum, I know!) contribute £ 1. 45 in economic output to the national economy. Imagine if all these impoverished British colonies generate £ 1. 45 billion annually and independently. Imagine if Pink nations actually pay or share these gains with Africa and Asia, the wounded and sapped victims. Imagine if your countries, dear descendants of the enslaved, have such museums: the Pinks will be flooding Africa and Asia for sightseeing or for artistic business, thereby elevating our cultures and boosting our separate economies. And if African countries are enriched by these stolen artefacts and other valuables belonging to us, do you think our brothers and sisters will still be trudging through deserts or dying in ships just to get to Pink people's countries to escape poverty? The answer, of course, is no. But, alas, we have lost our treasures to Pink beasts, and there is no promise of any gratitude (which is not all that we need!) or a return of all these looted goods, which is extremely exasperating!

Number Three says that this sector employs a minimum of 38, 165 people and it is made up of approximately 2, 635 organizations running 2, 720 sites across England.

God, this is an impressive fortune for the Pinks! The British Museum really owes us, their empire, swift gratitude because without those artefacts of ours which they looted and kept in this museum, there will be a substantial increase in Pink unemployment across the UK. The Pinks should be thankful. Thy should be remorseful. They should really be ashamed of their pathetic criminality. They should willingly return those valuables to us Africans and to other victims in Asia. I am extremely exasperated, because those whose stolen goods continually give other people jobs and keep them busy, healthy, wealthy and alive are hungry, suffering, drying and are often denied job opportunities in that very criminal museum.

Number Four says that the sector is estimated to generate £ 3 of income (including earned income, income from investments, grants from charities and foundations, and donations, etc) for each £ 1 of public sector grant. Imagine if Nigeria or any other robbed African nation has all these foundations and grants created from the gains of our cultural property? Do you think many of our ambitious youths will still be jobless and living in penury? The British Museum dealt with us seriously, and is still hurting us. And for this economic help our stolen goods have given to the British people, they owe us some gratitude.

CHAPTER NINE

SOLD SOULS, OH YE DESCENDANTS OF THE ENSLAVED

Dear African Brothers and Sisters: The journey from Africa to the Americas was one of the most inhuman experiences in history. Many of our brothers and sisters died because they were callously packed in the ships. There was limited food, but there were diseases. Whenever I seriously think about the Pinks, I remember the cold-blooded John Hawkins. This Pink devil, according to Walter Rodney in his groundbreaking book, *How Europe Underdeveloped Africa*, "made three trips to West Africa in the 1560s, and stole Africans whom he sold to the Spanish in America. On returning to England after the first trip, his profit was so handsome that Queen Elizabeth 1 became interested in directly participating in his next venture; and she provided for that purpose a ship named the Jesus."

Oh, ye descendants of the enslaved, this criminal named Hawkins was so encouraged that he left with the *Jesus* to steal some more Africans like chewing gum and returned to England with them and the Queen crowned his efforts by making him a knight. The stealing, oh ye descendants of the enslaved, did not end here. The expanded capitalist money enjoyed by Western Europe was good and silver mined by Africans. Rodney argues, and I agree, that African gold helped the Portuguese to finance further navigations around the Cape of Good Hope and into Asia ever since 15th century. And this enslavement, my brothers and sisters, have not ceased, though it has taken a different form. So, oh ye descendants of the enslaved, do not believe Pink people when they come to you to say that racism is overhyped these days or that it is (almost) dead. Tell them it isn't because it isn't. Racism is alive in every facet of our life in the West and other some other parts of the world. We find racism in:

1. Religions
2. Relationships
3. Sports
4. Movie and the industry
5. The Church
6. Publishing business
7. Academia
8. Politics

i. RELIGIONS

The Abrahamic religions – Christianity, Islam, and Judaism – have some benign and fabulous sides of them but one cannot pretend that their shared idea of God and Satan isn't racist.

Let me Explicate this, using Christianity, the one I am more familiar with, the one into which I was born and raised. The British who brought Christianity to Nigeria (and Africa, generally) made the people to believe, through their interactions and preaching, that God is a "white" man and Satan is a "black" rebel sent down from heaven. Of course, no human on Earth is white, but the British and other Pink Europeans call themselves white people and call us Blacks. They call us Blacks and call Satan Black. The same Bible they used – use – makes us to believe that no angel is black-coloured. And Satan was an angel. So, Satan should be called a white guy, and NOT described as black. I always ask, in anger: why is Satan suddenly lumped with Africans (the "Blacks") by these Christians? The answer is clear: "White", which they wrongly and politically call themselves, cannot identify with evil and ugliness, so Satan must be described as black, just like Africans. This political madness, this political wickedness and political insincerity, unfortunately, has stood uncorrected for centuries. Go to Nigeria, my country, or any other African nation, you will be shocked to discover that virtually all the people mentally and orally describe God as a white man and describe Satan and a black man. They describe Satan as a black man while calling themselves blacks. Even the educated ones think God is a white like the British and Satan is black like Nigerians, Kenyans, Ghanaians or any other "Black" nation. Isn't this a clear case of insanity?

Oh, ye enslaved souls, I don't think it is wrong for "white" people, or Pink people(for nobody is actually white) to describe their as "white", but it is foolishness on your part of you join them in celebrating this "whiteness" while racially identifying with Satan, the "black" rebel they have created to look like you.

By the way, let me state here that I do not believe that Europeans came to Africa and chained Africans away and enslave them. It is the narrative that the Europeans want the world to believe, to make themselves appear powerful. The European finger has controlled the narrative for a long time and this has sunk into everyone and that astonishing story has been seen as true.

I have come to tell you, that it is not true. However, I must warn you, for fact checking, which means that I have to rely on old materials written by Europeans, one will begin to question the source of my claim. I want to assure you that this version of my narrative, was passed on to me orally.

Did we write in Igbo land? Yes, we did. How?

Over 200 years ago, my great-great-grandfather, Nze Ukwu Nwelue Nnadum, was the Royal Court Adjudicator at the Palace of Eze Nsu. He was a great orator, which we see in the family lineage. He travelled widely, which we see today, as I have travelled to more than 80 countries.

Nze is a title in Igbo cosmology and caste system. It simply alludes to the Intellectuals and King Makers. What is important here, is to understand that there is no way, a European can come to a sophisticated society like the Igbo land and bundle anyone away without the complicity of the people. Achebe warned about the need for the lions to start telling the story of the hunt, lest the hunter conscripts all he tales. This is my own effort to wrestle with the lies and contrived narratives Europeans have spinned about us for centuries.

ii. RELATIONSHIPS

Racism is wide awake in all kinds of relationships in America, the United Kingdom and other Western countries. Interracial couples in countries where you, dear enslaved descendants are, still struggle with the effects of racism. It was not even long ago that loving someone from a different racial background was a crime in America. That was put to a stop by the Supreme Court in 1967. Few years before that, on August 28, 1955, a fourteen-year-old Emmett Till, an African American from Chicago, was brutally murdered for allegedly flirting with a white woman. A "white" person would rather marry another "white" person he hates than marry a "Black" person they genuinely love. These so-called "white" folks worry about what their families and friends would say if they bring you, oh dear enslaved descendants' home, as if you were a blood-sucking beast or some wild animal from the wood.

Consider this insightful extract from Gary John Herr's terrific dissertation, Factors Influencing Black-White Interracial Marriage Satisfaction (2009):

Among Black/White couples, the feelings of family, friends, and the general public are extremely important and influential. In one study of Black/White interracial couples (Killian, 2001), 80 % of the participants reported feeling personal pain and frustration from perceived negative public reactions to their relationship. Killian believes this emotional hurt represents a real consequence of racism and intolerance in our society and merits exploration in therapy. Fears of what others may think about interracial relationships also affect American dating relationships. Wang, Kao, and Joyner (2004) found that adolescents involved in interracial romances were less likely to reveal their relationships to their families and to the public eye, and were also less likely to meet their partner's parents. Wang et al. also reported that couples involved in interracial dating were more likely to terminate their relationships than their counterparts in intra-racial relationships.

French colonial officers from Ivory Coast with their
Ghanaian wives and children in Ghana in 1915.

During the colonial times in Africa, marriages
between colonial officers and African women were
not based on romance. Colonial powers created a new
generation of Africans who had many benefits than
full blooded Africans. They had opportunities such
as free education in Europe. Then they returned to
Africa and got administrative positions. Also, they
had sympathy for their European fathers. The main

reason was to serve the colonial powers and ease their presence.

Now, I want you, oh ye enslaved descendants, to ask yourselves this question: why do countless "white" folks rise to say, unabashedly, that All Lives Matter when racially abused and deprived Africans dating their brothers or sisters say Black Lives Matter? The answer is clear: they are racists!

iii. SPORTS

Oh ye, enslaved descendants, I think racism is salient and probably the worst in sports, particularly in football. Pink footballers racially abuse their African teammates because of their skin colour. There are constant cases of racist chants heard during matches in Italy, France, Spain, England, Germany, and so on. Oguchi Onyenwu, an American of Nigerian descent, has been attacked by fans while playing for Standard Liege because he is "black". Jelle Van Damme, a Pink Dutch guy, repeatedly called him a "dirty ape."

In January 2005, in Ligue 1, PSG's crowd in the kop of Boulogue sang "come on the whites", and was exacerbated by "monkey chants from the Boulogue crowd whenever a Lens player touched the ball.

In 1994, Borrusia Dortmund footballer Julio Cesar threatened to leave the club after he was refused admission to a local nightclub because of him being black.

In April 2009, Inter Milan's star Mario Balotelli, an Italian of Ghanaian descent, was subjected to racial abuse from Juventus fans while playing at UEFA Euro 2012. He fell to monkey chants during a match against Spain.

iv. MOVIES AND THE INDUSTRY

Oh ye descendants, you are not even safe in the movie industry. It is impossible to get most of the films of seminal filmmakers of colours; they do not promote them, do not celebrate them, do not rate them and certainly do not distribute them because Pink folks think that our lives do not matter, so watch them? Even the pathetically few movies "exploring" and "repressing" Blackness do it embarrassingly with the infuriating stereotypes.

On an *Screen Daily* news ("UK actors face widespread institutional racism at work, survey finds"), which was written by Orlando Partfitt on 24th April, 2021, he discloses an insignful research done with The Sir Lenny Henry Centre Media Diversity at Birmingham City University. They polled 1, 300 actors about their experiences with racism between March and April this year (2021). Among the key findings: 55 % of the respondents asserted that they have directly experienced racism in the workplace. 79 % conceded that thy felt roles continue to stereotype their ethnicities.

You might find this extract very interesting (and of course disturbing):

The research flagged up casting as a particular concern. 61% said they felt unable to turn down auditions that stereotype ethnicities, with 64% having experienced racist stereotyping in an audition.

Respondents said many casting briefs included racist stereotypes which lead to discriminatory behaviour at auditions, often managed by all-white panels. For example, code words were used in conjunction with stereotypes of African-Caribbeans stereotypes, with actors being told to 'play it more "sassy", "urban", and "street"; and actors of various ethnicities were asked to 'do a Middle-Eastern accent'.

During productions, 71% of participants said they had experiences of hair and make-up departments being unable to cater to their heritage, hair or skin tone; and 66% of respondents felt "generally" unable to discuss issues openly with a director.

This is an enormous cross for us to carry, oh ye enslaved descendants: because during productions of movies about the evils of racism there are cases of racism!

v. THE CHURCH

Perhaps this one is very obvious to most educated Christians, though they would not like to admit it. The church, I am bold to say, is one of the most racist institutions in the world. Perhaps I should say the Catholic Church, because they are the most political. Oh ye, descendants of the enslaved, have you ever seen a Pope who skin is like yours? The Catholic always chooses a "white" man to make a Pope; the idea of a "Black" man in Vatican perturbs them.

A few years ago, there was exciting news amongst (Catholic) Christians Nigeria because it was rumoured that Cardinal Arinze from Anambra State, Nigeria, a dark-skinned gentleman, would be made Pope. But I it never happened.

vi. PUBLISHING BUSINESS

The Western world, as we know, look down on us and expect the worst from us. This sense of superiority is the reason why they are not always keen on publishing books that celebrate the beauty or the rich cultures of Africa. A young writer from Africa who's desirous to have his or her book published in the West almost always chronicles deliberately exaggerated realities – corrupt politicians, barbarism, bribery, prowling lions and elephants and tigers, poverty, diseases, HIV/AIDS, etc. These are the kinds of narratives many Western publishers expect from "The Heart of Darkness"; they do not want you to sing your glorious, sing your blues, sing your joys. They want you, oh ye descendants of the enslaved, to sing their praises: how they always donate to Africa, how accept African refuges and give them better lives, how they give us Jesus, formal education and so on. I remember, in an interview, the Nigerian writer, Chimamanda Ngozi Adichie, narrated how her debut novel, *Purple Hibiscus,* was repeatedly rejected by American publishers. One of them actually questioned the authenticity of the story: Do Africans behave like this? They talk with civility, they drove cars and go to offices, they use electronic appliances, they behave just like him. How is this possible? To this stunned man, an African is an animal, a money perhaps, and not a real human being who can behave like him. He "advised" the young writer from Africa, Ngozi Adichie, to change the setting from Nsukka to a city in the US so that it could be acceptable, but she refused to be intimidated into believing that we, oh ye descendants of the enslaved, were sub-human. She won, as the book was eventually published elsewhere.

But there are several African or African American authors who could not win. Look at the stories and you will be saddened that many of the works are poverty porn. I wouldn't drop titles here; I just want you to go to a library and pick any African book written in our recent history.

vii. ACADEMIA

Within workplaces, Pink people discriminate and even disrespect Africans or "Black people", including the ones who are their superiors. Mind you, dear Pink people, racial discrimination is not only spewing disparaging or demeaning comments on the skin colour of an African colleague, but it is also evident in your subtle unwillingness to promote my brothers and sisters as swiftly as you do for your own people. Dr. Eddie Tembo quit as an academic because "as a black academic in a UK university, I became accustomed to defending myself to students and sometimes to staff." He has a doctorate, but he would always tell his skeptical Pink student's ,"No, it was not awarded to me to fill a quota" and at early career conferences he "encountered disbelief that I could have published a book. White colleagues seldom endured this sort of scepticism and it was enough to put me off conferences. I've had painful experiences at the hands of former colleagues, including the use of racist language and the overt propagation of racist stereotypes." He is, I feel I should inform you, in the police force in the United Kingdom.

More subtle racism was harder to deal with, such as sidelining (always hard to prove) or the use of strategic appointments – a modern variant of the old boys' club – to fill vacancies with strategic appointments through the helps or the very Pink old boys' club. And I also know that the negative effects of the Pinks' racism are worse to our brothers and sisters in the Western universities. I remember Zac Adan, a "Black" 19-year-old first-year student, when he was accuses of "looking like a drug dealer" by University of Manchester security officers; they held him up against a wall and demanded that he must produce his identification. It was very controversial. Nancy Rothwell, the vice chancellor, had to resign and later apologised for the false claims she made on national television: that she wrote to Adan to make an apology.

There are several other racial incidents, oh ye descendants of the enslaved, but I do not want to depress you with all these anecdotes.

iiv. POLITICS

No sane human being can shamelessly pretend that there is no racism in Western politics. Oh ye descendants of the enslaved, Pink folks do not want you in "their" Europe and in "their" America as equal citizens, let alone as their leaders. They cannot stand that. They have never been able to stand that. Remember that the presidents of all the European nations do not have the same skin colour as you. These presidents can be anything but "Black." This unmitigated racism or discrimination does not entail that we do not have intellectuals and born leaders who are capable to pilot the affairs of any Western country, but Pink folks, as I have said, cannot stand the idea of you, an African born by an African slave, to be their president. The United States of America, a country that has a substantial number of African Americans and Africans, had to wait for centuries before a non-Pink person, Barack Obama, was elected in 2008. Not that it was an easy ride. Obama, as I read on social media, in papers and heard from "white" Americans, wished death upon an innocent president; some Pink idiots even swore that he would be shot, as The White House, to them, is meant for "white" folks and not for "monkeys." It's a miracle that Barack Obama did him job admirably well and left The White House without being gunned down by some Pink bastards.

Having been reminded all these evils of the Pink people and their unmitigated racism, do you, oh ye descendants of the enslaved, need a soothsayer to tell you that they do not really care about you or think you are a full human being?

CHAPTER TEN

IS IT STOCKHOLM SYNDROME OR TRANS-GENERATIONAL TRAUMA?

African cinema may have left the realm of political ideological fruiting during colonial mobile cinema shows. African cinema with its seeming engagement with material beauty in the 21st Century, explores abstract realms of sensuality. It engages the material elements of story, but neglects utilitarian curiosity and fails deep seated folklore in our children's imaginations.

Otherwise, African folklore through moonlit village square absorption in the mental estate created by the griot or storyteller also passed distinctiveness. This was manifested in practiced visual or performance arts; which enthralled Europeans explorers of the so-called exotic Dark Continent!

Hardly exploring so called exotic essence, earlier sought after by Anglo-American curiosity, contemporary African cinema has evolved from a habitat of learning, absorbing and projecting nuanced lessons of moonlit stories into addiction on the opium of misled explorations of routine commerce.

There, ensued costly efforts to translate inter-lingual translation of verbal and non-verbal cinematic imagery between the colonized and colonized in colonial eras. Indeed, also the French colonial Europeanisation of African storytelling experience.

That authentic African storytelling estate was characterized by a children's show, *Tales by Moonlight*. It aired on Nigeria's National Television Authority (NTA)'s network for many years.

As it was traditional in moonlit village square,

grandparents' tales ended with the storyteller's underlining of essentials moral lessons. Such morals bequeathed a sense of communality and commonality of duties and obligations to society. The modern Israeli might lean on the biblical story of Abraham; but for African or Nigerian Igbo ethnicity, where I am from, it could be how to trade across international boundaries.

Lessons from NTA's Tales by Moonlight also included peaceful co-existence among Nigerian ethnic nationalities. And you begin to wonder, why there are still ethnic tensions in Nigeria in the year 2021. It would seem that such media stunts have failed to invest and harvest from an authentic mental estate. The perpetual flowering Nigerian disunity will be inherited by Nigerian young or X-generation.

We need to call out African nay Nigerian mass media from the trick of leisure and entertainment. We need to cultivate 21st Century African cinema storytelling on utilitarian paradigm. That is upholding authentic education for individual and collective survival through cinema culture: from conception to onscreen communication.

In earliest post-colonial times, Anglo-American cinema continued to impact subterranean cultural messaging that overpoweringly Americanized or

Anglicized African sensibilities. But the strongest impact is images more than dialogue, [1] because African audiences hardly read subtitles.

Therefore, from the joys of moonlit storytelling, which conveyed practiced Africanity to the urbanized African; more pitiable new-born and unknown generation, authentic African curiosity has long been lost to Anglo-Americanism or French cinematic ethos; depending on your shade of cultural colonization.

There occurs a precipitation of confusion in terms of sociopolitical economy, arising from cultural linguistic shift generally in community. So, remnants of Africanity struggle to authenticate culture, history, ethnicity and worship systems. That is how powerful contemporary 21st African cinema may have lost its authenticity; perhaps unlike the Asiatic Chinese or Indian cinematic identities.

You might say Nigeria's Nollywood having become, if not a global cinematic darling, but a commercial videographers' heaven has done enough in projecting African ethos. Howbeit French integration demonstrates the best of what I call cultural denudation of the average 21st Century African child's studying curiosity.

Ousmane Sembene reputedly the Father of African cinema[2] had his 1960s films struggling with balancing authentic African imagery with Europeanized or French cinematic mysteriousness for the African. He championed '…the right of the socially excluded and illiterate to vocalize his authenticity. Sembene's *Borom Sarret* and *Black Girl….*' for linguistic '…function and status…,' elucidated politics, which communicated the centrality of global English, French or American cultural conquests.

His efforts may have failed to counteract what Jonathan Haynes in his explanation; terms a historical lag. Because as soon as cinema got invented Africa embraced its global system '…on the most unfavorable terms…;' became the dumping ground for second-run "B" movies from Hollywood, Bollywood and Hong Kong, films that are often racist and always estranged from African realities and purposes.' [3]

This he opines comes from inability to match the, '… formidable technical, infrastructural, and capital requirements of making and distributing films…' And when Sembene responded with *Black Girl*, it was not possible in that kind of way.

This I believe him, keeps arising from dearth of infrastructural and capital capacity. These most often in the likes of South Africa's well-organized ala apartheid era foundations were and are still basically state supported. Therefore, capacity dearth in most African countries evidenced as Haynes posits indifferent, timid, corrupted and inept post-colonial elites.

Yes, he is right about that deluded cultural honeycomb that whets elites' appetites to remain ignorant of the essential impact of cinematic imageries on the young African mind. Really; a clear departure from biosocial and mental pastures created by moonlit storytelling in gradually lost African traditional storytelling-cine culture.

I consider the fact that Sembene in the process of enacting a counter praxis with an '... authentic subjective voice in a *prise de parole* (an act of speech or talking back) ...' saw a political need. He waited till 1968 to find his essential and authentic 'Africaphone' as opposed to Francophone....'

It was indeed a struggle, because he embraced the grill of linguistic mystification through versions of same movie, *Mandabi* (Wolof) and *Le Mandat* to stride that perceived cultural distance, the French sought to narrow , through assimilation. So, for such African filmmakers, wherever they are today it is *aluta continua*. Especially in Nigeria, where we vomit our confused cultural meals of Anglo-American and French influences to transliterate through European created boundaries. Really, to communicate our increasingly lost cultural estate among young hip-hoppers and the likes, who, delight in the religiosity of eroded Africanity.

Between 2020 and 2021 Netflix, Apple, Amazon, Hulu and many other gangling digital platforms have taken on such deluded African, nay Nigeria's Nollywood movie paradigms. They are keying into what Multichoice, a South African channel, perhaps authentic in the sense of its African origins has been doing since 1994. Yes, as a sports channel, another aspect of global enactment of Anglo-America or European cultural impact.

The name Multi-choice implies everything Ousmane Sembene's French producer Robert de Nelse demanded of him. Robert demanded universalism Sembene from; away from what he made of the filmmaker's as '...outdated political...' cinematic re-engineering of African biosocial storytelling estate; perplexed by that subterranean Anglo-American or French cinema. [4]

You might liken Sembene's authenticity clout to Nigeria's Nollywood authenticator flick, *Living in Bondagei*(1999) by Keneth Nnebue. Whose process of authentication embodied trading off empty CDs or DVDs, but inadvertently altering videography, vis-à-vis 'cinematic storytelling.'

Kenneth's authentication was market driven, compared to earliest Nigerian flick made by Geoffrey Barkas, *Palaver* (1926); first ever to feature Nigerians in speaking roles. I believe that the pre-colonial to immediate post-colonial era witnessed the primal confiscation of the Nigerian child's mental estate; fenced off from foreign depletion until the Portuguese landed in Benin Kingdom in 1432.

Prior to Nigeria's military indigenization decree in 1972, which legitimized the takeover of 300 film theatres, Herbert Ogunde and Moses Oliaya, Nigeria's prolific traditional stage-drama producers and actors transitioned into big screen shows. The 1970s oil boom boosted cinema culture, towards the dwindling 1980s to 1990s, when Nigerians found escape from oil-boom punishment of national recklessness with comic dramas like Wale Adenuga's *Papa* Ajasco(1984) *Mosebolatan*(1985) by Moses Olaiya.

Of course, the mid-1970s through mid-1980s markedly referred as the Golden Age of Nigerian cinema, pushed forward that market experiment via Kenneth Nnebue's *Living Bondage*. It enacted superstition as a driver of Nigerian survival in economic misfortunes of many urbanites.

It becomes imperative to examine Nigerian cinema vis-à-vis the Nigerian society; indeed, through the historical nuances of the cinema industry itself. Let's see that relationship through the lens of video-cinema culture, which may have denuded or enhanced Africanity in contemporary times.

There was the very omnipresent **Golden Age 1950s- 1980s; including Anti-Colonialism 1950s-1960s.** The period marked Nigeria's earliest film screenings on August 12, 1903. In 1913 British South African Company made short documentary series on *Jos Countryside and Tin Mines*; to document the socio-political economy of solid mineral.

In 1949 Nigeria's earliest best-known documentary, *Daybreak in Udi,* by Terry Bishop designed on Colonial Office's progress in the health sector portrayed implementation of community projects in Eastern Nigeria. [5]

Palaver(1926)by Geoffrey Barkas; filmed amongst the Sura and Angas people of the Bauchi Plateau in Northern Nigeria, show-cased rivalry between a British District Officer and a tin miner; leading to war.

Sanders of the River (1935) by Zoltán Korda, featured Sanders, British colonial District Commissioner in Colonial Nigeria fair treatment African Peoples of the River province. He gains native's respect; but is feared by some. A native literate ally, Bosambo's wife kidnapped in the wake of false rumor that Sanders is dead, while on leave prompts heroic Sanders' capture of the kidnappers. Basomba kills evil King Mofobola, the villain.

Fincho (1957) by Sam Zebba, first Nigerian film shot in color film dealt with the tension between Traditional and Innovation, and Mechanization's threat to Traditional Labor. The titular character epitomized industrialization brought to Nigeria by Europeans Colonialists.

The **Golden Age** also featured Hubert Ogunde's *Aiye, Ayanmo*; Ola Balogun's *Amadi, Cry for Freedom* and Moses Olaiya shot *Mosebolata*n. Jab Adu came with *Bisi: Daughter of the River,* while Isola Ladi Ladebo produced Vendor.

Through **Pre-1960s-Early-1970s, Ethnic Nationalism/Civil War** spelled out its remarkable filmmaking or film-going culture. Hubert Ogunde, , Aiye, Ayanmo, Ola Balogun, Ade Folayan, Jab Adu, Isola Ogunsola, Ladi Ladebo featured with titles listed earlier; including Ossie Davis' *Son of Africa*, and *Kongi's Harvest*.

The period also presented Sanya Dosumu's - *Dinner with the Devil;* Sadiq Balewa- *A Packet Of Chin-chin;* Wole Soyinka's *Blues for a Prodigal;* plus Eddie Ugbomah's *The Rise and Fall of Dr. Oyenusi, The*

Mask, Oil Doom, Vengeance of the Cult, Death of a Black President.

Post-civil Nigerian eager to pursue the 3Rs, Reconciliation, Reconstruction and Re-integration in Oil Boom and Doom Mid-1970s- Late-1980 showcased.

Ola Balogun - *Ajani Ogun* - *Musik*- Man, *Ija Ominira*; Adamu Halilu -*Shaihu Umar*

Video Film Era-late 1980s/Early 1990s-Mid-2000s featured Ade Ajiboye - *Soso Meji*; Ade Ajiboye –*Ekun*;

Kenneth Nnebue - *Living in Bondage, Glamour Girls*; Tunde Kelani - *Thunder Bolt; Dangerous Twins*; Tade Ogidan, *Madam Dearest*; Kunle Afolayan – *Irapa, The Figurine.*

Tony Abulu shot *Doctor Bello*; Michelle Bello - *Flower Girl*, while Biyi Bandele made *Half of a Yellow Sun*. Remi Vaughn Richards flicked *The Department*.

A so called **New Nigerian Cinema –Mid-2000s till date** has dated cinema raves *Fifty, Chief Daddy, Wedding Party 1 & 2; Banana Island Ghost, The CEO , '76, The Arbitration and sSuru L'ere.*

King of Boys, 93 Days, When Love Happens Again, Merry *Men: The Real Yoruba Demons* etc.

Izu Chukwu's '76 bears the mark of Classic Nigerian Cinema 21st Century theme.

As you may know Nigeria has achieved and has been celebrated but the bottom-line is commerce has invaded the mental storytelling African cinema real estate. It is obvious in the progressive or would you agree degenerating thematic encapsulation of Africanness; especially in the so-called New Cinema Era. But Izu Chukwu, a 'classicist' among other the likes of Kunle Afolayan's with *October 1*, acclaimed after America's Stephen Spielberg, seek to a bespoken Nigerian reality with '76. Perhaps a departure from bubble-gum, sometimes erotic and abstract flicks of the 21st Century.

The 21st Century Nigerian cinema goers have choice of eating popcorn, when bored in movie theatres. They could laugh and forget their worries intoned by the parlance, '*I won't come and kill myself....*' That manifest mental estate has subsisted in hit movies like *Wedding Party 1* and *2,* with its authentic celebratory Lagos party crowd show-off; yet devoid of storytelling. Such reflections have occurred in *King of Boys, Purple Hisbiscus,* but somewhat tempered in *Up North*.

These compared to '*76* or *Figurine* among other culture or political bottom-lined movies have more or less marked Africa, nay Nigeria's embrace of what informed Sembene's critiquing of so-called *calabash* cinema.

This by approach in style of classic tropes of rich, griot, and oral storytelling heritage guided by Western art cinema tradition got castigated. It insinuates the loss of that authentic African mental cinema real estate. It clearly provokes the question, what should be the politics of voice and language to impact urbanized confusion in African cinema imagery. [6] Or is it that the stripping of Africa's storytelling mental estate has come of age, like those of the Indian, Chinese or Micronesian cinema landscapes?

What is the place of the African arts cinema in defining its commercial cinema, indeed authenticating the aesthetic qualities of tone, volume, timbre, intonation and accents apart from the physiology of characters, inundated by realities of authentic locations?

James S. Williams' *Ethics and Aesthetics in Contemporary African Cinema, The Politics of Beauty (2019) is of the following opinion.*

"I wish to suggest ultimately that in films which set out to explore the material and cross-cultural opacity of language by subjecting it to different tensions, the screen itself becomes an echo chamber for a range of forms of sound, from the verbal

and musical to gradations of both silence and noise, raising
far-reaching questions about materiality and relationality in
African cinema that relate also to the visual image."

He goes on about interlingual embrace of auditory beauty, crossing all borders and generic, conceptual, national, ideological, political picture framed collection of a wonder of listening encounter.

He culminates his findings in Sembene's strategy of 'imperfection,' devoid Anglo-American or European pretense. Embodied in intellectual or peasant identity and clarifying the life action character; really, an authenticated subjective African cinematic imagery. [7]

I submitted that if we persist in the abstract perfection of deluded eroticism and materialism, we will never tell the real African moon-lit stories that authenticated the realities of the past, now needing pursuance of our development realities, there will never be an authentic African film.

CHAPTER ELEVEN

CHRIS KIRKLAND THINKS KICKING A CAT IS WORSE THAN RACISM

Just as I was finalising this text a pivotal event occurred in the UK. While I had tangentially raised the point in the introduction of this book, I did not feel like there was a practical example I could point to that is publicly known. This incident I am referring to is that of Kurt Zouma, an African born in France, thus a French citizen and who plays professional football for West Ham in the English Premier League. Sometime in February 2022, Zouma was filmed kicking his cat by his brother, who was stupid enough to upload it on social media. But as soon as it debuted on snapchat,

British citizens, and other Europeans most probably were horrified by the image of a defenceless cap being violently shoved in the air and getting living daylight kicked out of it. Expectedly, this drew widespread criticism from the British press and public who began to call for Zouma to be punished. However, it was the next day, after he was featured in a football match that the criticism suddenly took a different dimension, and revealed, in my understand, the ugly intersections of race, identity and nationality.

First, we may need to establish what the facts of the case was from in order to be able to deduce when and how nationality cannot save an African if the structures of racism and in-group identification still exists. Indeed, Zouma had made the grievous mistake of not recognizing the burden of the sojourner. The sojourner must remain conscious of the laws and norms of his host, lest he not only angers them, but run the risk of bringing his/herself to ruin. He should have known that you cannot kick your cat or act violently towards it. I don't even know why people own pets. I think it is wicked to enslave an animal under the pretext of loving. Animals are freest in their own habitat; except we also wish to argue that humans can enjoy being loved as caged pets whose freedoms reside with their owners. Anyway, by capturing and uploading the incident online, Zouma's brother unwittingly set him up for a national stone-pelting contest. What seemed like the nail on the young man's coffin was that his West Ham football club, rather than announce a punishment for him (even if for performative purposes) were satisfied with his public apology and then selected him for a game. A national outcry thus erupted in the wake of this.

The reactions however were so overboard, it became apparent that people may no longer be responding out of sorrow for the cat, but as part of some pent-up anger and desire to destroy an African and his source of livelihood. There was quickly a petition to relieve him of his job. The swiftness with which 150,000 signatures were assembled was not only terribly frightening. Vitality UK, one of the main sponsors of Zouma's club withdrew their partnership with the club. Quickly also, Adidas who had a sponsorship deal with the player terminated his contract. The club then docked his wages for 2 weeks which was in the tune of 300,000 GBP which they pledged to an animal rights charity. Zouma's cat had by then been taken away from him to pet shelter. But the British were not done with him just yet. The animal rights protection group - PETA wrote to the club's majority owner, David Sullivan to fire the player. In her words,

> "Anyone who abuses an animal in such a heinous way must suffer the consequences for their actions. To allow Zouma to continue to play for your club would be a stain on West Ham's reputation and would send a worrying message to your fans and the public that the club doesn't take animal abuse seriously."

Interestingly, Chris Kirkland, a former goalkeeper for England produced the most skating and bizarre response to the incident. In arguing for Zouma to receive the worst punishment possible, he advocated for the Football Association in England to step in and boot Zouma out because what the player had done was worse than racism. It is important in fact, to reproduce Kirkland's exact words, which is:

> "Everywhere he goes, he's going to be targeted and rightly so as well because he deserves everything he's going to get. I'm a big advocate for mental health and I need to

be careful with what I say because it is going to test Kurt Zouma. But he brough it upon himself. But again, for me...if it was a racism case, the FA has stepped in and banned players 6-10 games, biting, 6-10 games. This is worse, if anything. What is the difference?"

Kirkland's rambling above is not simply that he foolishly comes to one of the most-watched programmes in Britain - BBC Breakfast to say that kicking a cat was worse than racism; it is that it made any sense to him at all. Expectedly, there was a lot of push-back and criticism aimed at him, especially from the African population, who understands that the retired goalie wasn't just speaking for himself, but that his views (which were both insensitive and racist) was not slip of the tongue, but the way many Caucasian British people feel about Africans.

Now let us go to the outcry from the British public, which surprisingly is never there when an African player is racially abused. When Patrice Evra was racially abused by Luiz Suarez and Anton Ferdinand by John Terry, the outcry was never there. The petition to relieve these players of their jobs were never there. In fact, some people felt pity for

John Terry who retired from international football after the FA stripped him of his captaincy's position in the team. It is therefore not a surprise that years later, Mr. Kirkland would equate the kicking of a cat to the casual misdemeanor of racial abuse. It is really unfortunate because football games in the English Premier League are all preceded by taking a knee to show solidarity against racism. This has caused some serious debate on whether it is justified or a needless virtue signaling. Well, why does it matter if it changes very little in the attitude of the majority in Britain who may just be fuming that such a gesture exists at all. In short, it is possible that this may have built up a pent-up rage, which the British public had waited to use on the first African that makes a mistake. True, Zouma had breached social norms in the country of his residence, where he works and earns enormous wages for kicking a ball, yet, it was a mistake for which he had apologized for. The cat in question did not die, and was subsequently taken from him. His wages had been docked, and his lucrative Adidas sponsorship had been cancelled. Was this not punishment enough? How could people further clamour for his livelihood to be taken away from him, when the same treatment was now called for those who racially abused African players in the very country?

Let us also consider the case of Adidas, whom despite Luiz Suarez's use of racial slur and two incidents of biting fellow players (Branislav Ivanovic and Giorgio Chiellini) during in football games, Adidas never cancelled his contract, nor suspended him. It is scandalous that Adidas had no time nor shame to confront the reality of their own hypocrisy and double standards and racism. Just like Kirkland, racism seemed much easier for them to condone than an African kicking a cat. My major takeaway from the incident remains that Africans must understand that the mere fact that they were born in a corner of Europe and thus, holders of a European passport does not change how majority of the society feels about you. Yet more Africans arrive Europe or America or Canada each year, pay their dues in these societies and in due course are rewarded with citizenship. A great deal of them are then quick to believe that they are one with their host, but if there is one thing I can always bet on for pink people, it is their ability to disenchant the hallucinatory minds of these 'settled' migrants, that although they hold the country's passport, they are not one of them. Of course, race is one thing. Nationality is another thing. Those who conflate the two, just like Zouma, always find out the hard way.

THE REAL OWNERS
OF BRITAIN

When I moved to Oxford, as an Academic Visitor at the African Studies Centre, University of Oxford, I screened my biopic of Emeka Ojukwu, on November 4th, 2021 at Lincoln College.

When I stood there to give my speech, I could visualise myself as Shashi Tharoor, speaking at the Oxford Union Society, of which I joined much later as a member.

Mr. Tharoor is one of the most brilliant men I know, and I thought, his brilliance shone through and would anyone be as eloquent and gracious?

I could try with my speech at the screening of *Other Side of History*, which was jampacked.

I will reproduce the speech I gave that very night here.

Let me begin by thanking Professor Perry Gauci, or that gracious introduction. I am immensely grateful to you and to Lincoln College for hosting this event, and for your enormous contribution to this project.

I also want to thank distinguished members of the Nigerian Oxford University community who are present, including those who made concerted efforts to be here, even after tickets to this event had sold out. I am speaking, specifically, of course, of Professor Kingsley Moghalu, who has emerged in recent years as a fresh, energetic, insightful and inspirational voice in the Nigerian political landscape.

And I will be remiss if I did not mention how interesting it is that I am running my programme here at Oxford at the same time as both Professor Moghalu and his former boss, HRH Lamido Sanusi Lamido, 14th Emir of Kano, who is currently a fellow at St. Antony's College.

To Professor James Currey, an immensely generous benefactor and spiritual forebear in many ways, words do not suffice to show my gratitude to you.

I'm also delighted to see special friends of mine, including the new ones that I've made here at Oxford in recent weeks; as well as the extraordinary individuals who have made this journey with me; and so many others of you.

Your presence here, all of you, fills me with great pride.

In 1982, 'Emeka', the pioneering literary title that captures the fascinating evolution of Dim Chukwuemeka Odumegwu-Ojukwu, was published. Veteran journalist and celebrated novelist, Frederick Forsyth, who authored Emeka, chose that title based on his reflections on the emotional intimacy he observed between Ojukwu and the Igbo people of the then breakaway Republic of Biafra during the Nigerian Civil War. Emeka was the endearing name that Igbos chose to refer to Ojukwu as during the war.

Coincidentally or not, the publication of this biography was well-timed: 1982 was, after all, the same year that Ojukwu returned to Nigeria from exile in Cote d'Ivoire. This confluence of events afforded him the opportunity to stamp his own impression on this largely definitive work on his life's story. In the foreword to 'Emeka', Ojukwu writes, quite candidly and pointedly:

Much has been written about me over the past fifteen years, and a great deal of it has been, alas, quite inaccurate. None of it was written with my personal authority.

In the trailer for the Other Side of History, this statement is verbally rendered as an appropriate introduction to the different bits of history that form a rounded whole in dramatizing the private life of Ojukwu.

I recall that many years ago, while reading the aforementioned book by Forsyth, some paragraphing which struck me as tantalizing became engraved in my memory bank, and these were in particular, bits of peculiar information about Chukwuemeka Ojukwu's evolution. I reproduce the excerpt at length for emphasis:

> For one thing he (Emeka) had a handsome allowance from his father, which enabled him to dress in the most elegantly cut suits and drive a series of newest and fastest British sports cars. He was observed by contemporaries to be seldom out of the company of a string of very attractive young women.
>
> Then there were the parties, the weekend trips to London and the high life of the capital. It was probably the social life that cost him a place in the Oxford Rugby team of his final year. He made his place as wing three-quarter in the London College team... But to make a place in the university Rugby team meant a ruthless dedication to a course

of extreme physical fitness. That in turn meant a
choice between physical training or late-night parties
and lively social life. The social life won.

At the time, I conceived no deliberate mental picture
to those words, let alone contemplate a biopic to
popularize them. But I did not forget them either. And
as it turns out, nine years ago, I was again tantalized
by what seemed a salacious prompt on my phone
one languid Saturday afternoon. It was the headline
of a special report by Uduma Kalu for Vanguard
Newspaper, one of Nigeria's leading media outfits,
and It was captioned thus: **Ojukwu: Sexcapades of the**
Biafran Leader.

I remember letting out an inquisitive and slightly
audible sigh, 'hmm'—not for any lewd reason, but
because I felt a rush of allure, good enough to make me
want to click on the prompt. I paused for a moment,
looked at the prompt again, and clicked on it. The rider
to the caption, which by the way was rather short, read:
"*Had four wives, romantic poems and controversial marriages'*.
Interestingly, unlike the seemingly passive experience
I had whilst reading the passage excerpted above from
the book by Forsyth, this time, I made a mental note
of this short summary, and, by the time I was done
reading the report, a varied, creative kaleidoscope

began to take shape in my mind's eye. And so, for the first time, I began to conceive this grand picture of Ojukwu that was in sharp contrast to the avalanche of projectiles, hand grenades, explosions, Saracen tanks, unsmiling soldiers, spectacles of wartime oratory, and so on – motifs which occupy and still dominate the popular imagination of the man. This is the crucible in which what I believe the theme of this film to be, *the inversion of bellicosity*, was formed.

It was after this sudden epiphany of the interconnectedness of these tantalizing details—from Forsyth to Vanguard—that I began to actively consider a potential biopic in Ojukwu's name. And in a flash of a more stimulating illumination, the profound words of the philosopher Karl Jaspers wafted through my mind, chiming in this manner: *'however minute a quantity the individual may be in the factors that make up history, he is a factor'*.

Instinctively, I felt a rush to situate these hallowed words within the mode of individual peculiarities. I therefore resolved to focus not only on this individual—who was by no means minute in the history of post-colonial Nigeria and indeed Africa, but whom most of us had somehow come to consign to a mental box marked 'the generalissimo of the Biafran people'—but to highlight he was also —and in fact more so—a wealthy, libertine, gregarious, Oxford-nurtured fellow.

What the *Other Side of History* represents and intends to achieve is the mainstreaming of that side of the same coin which has suffered oblivion for too long. It is by no means a portrayal of the totality of the manifold inherences of Chukwuemeka Ojukwu, but it is an artistic effort in the promotion of balance, in stimulating those sentimental sensibilities, borne out of idiosyncrasies, that also colour the ways in which many of history's resonant figures come to be viewed, for better or for worse.

As many here will know, the young Ojukwu graduated from Lincoln College in 1955 with a degree in Modern History. The degree itself was a rebellious pursuit which his iron-willed father, Sir Louis Odumegwu-Ojukwu, Nigeria's first billionaire, did not approve at the outset. The young Ojukwu was sent to Oxford by his father to study Law, which was more in vogue at the time, but he chose Modern History instead. Ojukwu was well-moulded academically, but enjoyed an unparalleled social life while he was here, and, as he would later disclose to Forsyth, 'his three years at Oxford were the happiest of his life'. Whilst here, he drove the latest luxurious cars that Britain had to offer, enjoyed a copious amount of social life and nightlife, mostly in the company of other young socialites.

When he returned to Nigeria in 1955, he returned with an exquisite British accent, and, as he would later attest to, an extensive wardrobe of impeccably cut English suits and a sundry collection of high-class supercars. As a wealthy, smooth-speaking young man with glowing skin, Ojukwu became the cynosure of young ladies in Nigeria, and as you would see in Other Side of History, he left no room for doubt that he was a thoroughgoing Casanova. Oxford also bequeathed to him a consciousness on Africa, groomed from his membership of the Oxford West African Students Union. With Africa on the cusp of decolonization at the time, unions like that helped animate an apprehension among Africans studying in western universities about the continent's future. Little surprise then that Ojukwu was inspired to return early to Nigeria so he could serve his home country. Again, on this, he and his father disagreed. And yet again, his will triumphed over his father's as he eventually joined the Nigerian Army.

In Other Side of History, which covers Ojukwu's life in the years before Nigeria's independence, that is, between 1954 to 1960, viewers will be treated to an intimate portrayal of the much-vaunted poetic side of

Ojukwu, which he charmingly deployed in wooing the women he encountered during his lifetime. His equanimous voice, exotic accent, thrilling oratory, and urbane mannerisms were all attributes of someone worthy of the appellation of a Poète Romantique. Ojukwu's romance poetry was deemed head-spinning by those who were close to him, and Greg Ojefua—famous Nigerian thespian and protagonist playing Ojukwu in this film—has done a remarkable job of bringing that to life.

The film also features several acts portraying Ojukwu's Nigerian contemporaries and friends across the literary, entertainment and political domains like the dramaturgist, poet, and first African to win the Nobel Prize in Literature, Wole Soyinka; the preeminent Nigerian writer, Chinua Achebe; the extraordinary Nigerian poet who died fighting for Biafra during the civil war, Christopher Okigbo; the extremely talented Nigerian playwright and poet, John Pepper Clark; the First President of Independent Nigeria, Nnamdi Azikiwe; former Military Head of State and later President of Nigeria, Olusegun Obasanjo; former Military Head of State Yakubu Gowon; the first Black African to win a Gold Medal at an international sports event, Emmanuel Ifeajuna; the Ghanaian highlife pioneer, Emmanuel Tettey

(E.T.) Mensah, among others. Other side of History has made the first attempt ever to portray these people and the private relationship they all shared with Ojukwu as clearly and enjoyably as possible. In its portrayal of these highly consequential figures in Nigeria's history, the film moves beyond being a literary device intended to partially refocus audiences' consciousness on the less regarded traits of a great man, to becoming a story of friendship, of youthful idealism and exuberance, and of pristine aspirations eventually arrested by the disruptive and gruesome crosscurrents of post-colonial African statehood.

I would also venture to say that Other Side of History is a portrayal of an odd story of competing egos coexisting with filial love. This may be speculation, but I'm inclined to think that among the fruits of Chukwuemeka Ojukwu's defiance of his father at critical points in his youth was an abiding desire to match or even outdo the old man wherever possible. Having trod the path of military service, Chukwuemeka could not have matched his father in the department of industry and commerce. So, he settled for the only area where he enjoyed massive comparative advantage: women. Sir Louis married four wives, and Chukwuemeka would match his father in that department before exiting the scene.

ACKNOWLEDGEMENTS

I spent time at the Bodlean Library at the University of Oxford, reading through texts and encapsulating materials that helped in shielding this book. I am most grateful to Dr. Wale Adebanwi, Dr. David Pratten and Dr. Miles Larmer, for making it possible for me to join African Studies Centre.

Thank you to Mitterand Okorie, Ikenna Okeh, Ebelenna Esomnofu Ebelenna, Chinedu Vincent Okoro, Adepoju Isaiah Gbenga, MacDonald Ukah, Raphael Adebayo and Ifeanyi Mojekwu, whose contributions to this book are very much cherished.

The folks at Abibiman Publishing are amazing.

I thank Oluchukwu Chukwunyere Benneth (Duke), for everything. You don't see much of his person these days. Grateful to Obiora Anoze, Daniel Mbamala, Chinedu Ohiaeri, Chike Odigie and the others who continue to support me.

Thanks to everyone who committed their time and money to my projects.

BIBLIOGRAPHY

ActionAid International. (November 27, 2020). *How Shell is devastating the Niger Delta.* https://actionaid.org/stories/2020/how-shell-devastating-niger-delta

Anti-slavery. (n.d.). *What is modern slavery?* https://www.antislavery.org/slavery-today/modern-slavery/

BBC. (n.d). *Globalization.* https://www.bbc.co.uk/bitesize/guides/zxpn2p3/revision/5

Casely-Hayford, Adelaide. "Mista Courifer." *Blackboard.com.* n.d., Web. https://jsums.blackboard.com/bbcswebdav/pid-839359-dt-content-rid

Catalyze. (2018). *10 Things To Know About Cambridge Checkpoint.* https://www.catalyzecenter.com/blog/2018/may/10-things-to-know-about-cambridge-checkpoint.html

Dambisa, Moyo. (2009).*Why Foreign Aid is Hurting Africa.* https://econ4life.com/assets/why-foreign-aid-is-hurting-africa.pdf

Fanon, Frantz. (1967). *Black Skin, White Masks.*

trans. Richard Philcox. New York: Grove Press, p. 104.

Ibid., 105

Ibid., 103

Golebiewski, Daniel. (2014). *Religion and Globalization: New Possibilities, Furthering Challenges* retrieved on 17/01/2022 from https://www.e-ir. info/2014/07/16/religion-and-globalization-new-possibilities-furthering-challenges/

Henry Louis Gates Jr. (1988) "Foreword to Six Women's Slave Narratives" *The Schomberg Library of Nineteenth-Century Black Women Writers.* New York: Oxford University Press, p. xviii.

IndustriALL Global Union. (December 5, 2018). *Shell's hidden shame- Contract workers on poverty line in Nigeria.* https://www.industriall-union.org/shells-hidden-shame-contract-workers-on-the-poverty-line-in-nigeria

Mark, Monica. (2018). *Inside The Country Where You Can Buy A Black Man For $400.* https://www. buzzfeednews.com/article/monicamark/slavery-nigeria-libya

Moure, Miranda. (July 20, 2020). "9 famous stolen artifacts that are still in display in museums today". *Matador Network.* https://matadornetwork. com/read/stolen-artifacts-museums/

Obukohwo, Jenny. (2021). *How Mkpuru Mmiri was introduced to Nigerian youths by Mexican drug cartels retrieved on 17/01/2022 from* https://thestreetjournal. org/how-mkpuru-mmiri-was-introduced-to-nigerian-youths-by-mexican-drug-cartels/

Okeja, Uchenna. (2017).*The moral challenge of expatriate employment in developing countries.* https:// www.ntnu.no/ojs/index.php/etikk_i_praksis/article/ view/1985/2252

Okoro, Chinedu. (2020). *Dear Makonna* retrieved on 18/1/2022 from https://www.activemuse.org/2020_ short_stories/Chinedu_Okoro.html

Olson, Stephen. (2020). *Are private Chinese companies really private? Retrieved on*17/01/2022 *from* https://www.hinrichfoundation.com/research/article/ us-china/private-chinese-companies/

Pakenham, Thomas. (1991). *The Scramble for Africa.* UK: Random House.

Parfitt, Orlando. (August 24, 2021). "UK actors face widespread institutional racism at work, survey finds". *ScreenDaily.* https://www.screendaily.com/ news/uk-actors-face-widespread-institutional-racism-at-work-survey-finds/5162676.article

Peterson Institute for International Economics. (August 24, 2021). *What is Globalization? And How Has the Global Economy Shaped the United States? Retrieved on 24/01/2022 from* https://www.piie.com/microsites/ globalization/what-is-globalization

Rodney, Walter. (1974). *How Europe Underdeveloped Africa.* UK: Bogle-L'Ouverture Publications.

Singh, Bhupinder. (August 3, 2021). "9 Most Valuable Things Stolen By The British From India And Other Countries". *India Times.* https://www. indiatimes.com/amp/trending/social-relevance/ valuable-things-stolen-by-the-british-546394.html

Tampa, Vava. (2019). *Should the term 'black' to describe people of African origin be retired?* https://www. trtworld.com/opinion/should-the-term-black-to-describe-people-of-african-origin-be-retired-29105

The Editors of Encyclopaedia Britannica. (n.d.). *abolitionism.* https://www.britannica.com/ topic/abolitionism-European-and-American-social-movement

Tweyman, Stanley(ed.).(1994). *David Hume: Critical Assessments.* Routledge, p.381.

UKEssays. (July, 2021). *Positive and Negative effects of Globalization retrieved on 20/01/2022 from.* https:// www.ukessays.com/essays/economics/positive-and-negative-effects-of-globalisation-for-business-economics-essay.php

Wa Thiong'o, Ngugi. (1986). *Decolonizing the Mind.* London: James Currey Ltd, p.31.

Williams, James S. (2019). Ethics and Aesthetics in Contemporary African Cinema; The Politics of Beauty; London: Bloomsbury Publishing, p. 3.

- p.14
- p.142
- p. 143
- p.154

Xenia Madelin Bonilla. (2016). *The Effects of Globalization on Developing Countries retrieved on 18/1/2022 from* https://medium.com/@BonillaXM/the-effects-of-globalization-on-developing-countries-1e465257c4

Youmatter. (October, 2020). *Globalization: Definition, Benefits, Effects, Examples – What is Globalization?* https://youmatter.world/en/definition/definitions-globalization-definition-benefits-effects-examples/

Lightning Source UK Ltd.
Milton Keynes UK
UKHW041102300322
400833UK00003B/782